FOXTROT RIDGE

A BATTLE REMEMBERED

Also by the author . . .

*Unheralded Victory: The Defeat of the Viet Cong and the
North Vietnamese Army, 1961-1973*

FOXTROT RIDGE

A BATTLE REMEMBERED

BY
MARK W. WOODRUFF

VANDAMERE
PRESS

Published by
Vandamere Press
P.O. Box 17446
Clearwater, FL 33762
USA

ISBN 0-918339-58-8

CONTENTS

PREFACE

It is May 28, 2001, as I write these words: the 33rd anniversary of the battle of Foxtrot Ridge. Manuscripts have to be submitted to publishers months in advance of their planned release date and so I am writing this now. Despite the calendar indicating the year 2001, there's a part of me that always will exist, frozen in time, back on this date in 1968. This book is about the events that took place back then, and which had so much impact upon all of us who were there. I hope it does something to recognize the spirit, the humanity, and the bravery of those who were there. I am proud to say that I was one of the Marines who participated in the battle of Foxtrot Ridge described in this book.

I am staggered and humbled at the generosity and the support I was given in writing this account. Sometimes I was able to contact people by e-mail and give them a "heads up" about my wish to interview them. Often, though, I simply phoned them, completely unannounced, telling them that we served together 30 years ago and I wanted to talk to them about this battle. I live in Australia, which compounded the problems of communication. In Australia, we are 12 hours to 16 hours "ahead" of the relevant U.S. time, depending on which part of the USA you live. I had to calculate the time difference and coordinate our times. I often got it wrong. For various reasons, including confusion about time zone, changes in daylight savings, but mainly just my own mistakes, I sometimes phoned at totally wrong times and sometimes at great inconvenience to whomever I was phoning. I was met by overwhelming good humor and cooperation, however. Typical of this process was my phoning Jim Chafin. We had arranged (via e-mail) that I would phone him at 9:30 in the evening, his time.

Well, I got it horribly wrong and wound up phoning him at 1:30 in the morning, some four hours off-schedule. His wife (Sandy), sound asleep by that late hour, answered the phone, and when she realized who I was (Jim had been awaiting my call before finally giving up and going to bed himself), woke him up and handed him the phone. Of course I apologized profusely and said I'd phone in a day or two if he'd forgive me, but Jim just laughed and said, "No problems. Let's talk now." He proceeded to joke and laugh about the "good old days," while also providing extremely useful factual details about the battle in his sector. For others, recounting what took place was clearly painful, and something they had never done before. Again, their eagerness to help me in my effort to chronicle the battle was inspiring. Billy Cooper, who, probably out of modesty, declined to be interviewed for this book, was enormously helpful in tracking down and locating former Marines who fought at Foxtrot Ridge.

I started off planning to write a standard "third-person narrative" account of the battle (as I had done in *Unheralded Victory**), but I soon became enamored of the truth and realism of each veteran's own recounting of the events *in his own words*. I have tried to capture those words in this account. Each of the interviews was tape-recorded and transcribed as accurately as I could. Spoken English is quite different from written English, with the latter being far more formal. Most of us use far more colloquial English in our everyday conversations and generally shy away from the bigger words, which seem so pretentious when spoken. I say all of this because I have presented here the spoken words by these people. It is easy to criticize their grammar when presented in a written form, but the reader is advised to do so with caution. Remember, these were oral interviews, transcribed into verbal renditions. Similarly, I was hugely impressed by the diversity and rich regional differences of the way these people spoke. I tried to capture this as much as possible by writing their words as much as possible just as they were spoken. This approach leads to regional and geographic variations in English grammar. The only changes I have made are those wherein the interviewee referred to me in the second person (e.g., "We saw what was happening to you

---

*Mark W. Woodruff, *Unheralded Victory: Defeat of the Viet Cong and North Vietnamese Army, 1961–1973* (Arlington, Virginia: Vandamere Press, 1999)

guys on the ridge.") and I have changed this to the third person (e.g., "We saw what was happening to those guys on the ridge.") for consistency in the text.

I have included myself as an interviewee. I did so with much reluctance and uncertainty. In previous writings I have scrupulously omitted my own presence. It seemed appropriate to do so when I was writing "traditional" narrative history. In the case of Foxtrot Ridge, though, I was presented with a dilemma. There were fewer than 100 of us. I made every effort to locate and include as many veterans of that battle as possible. Why shouldn't I apply the same criteria to seeking out my own recollections? To omit my recollections would seem as if I was not as prepared to "bare my soul" as were my fellow Marines whose words fill this book. However, there was also a risk that I would appear to be aggrandizing my own minor actions and contributions to the battle. It seemed to me to be a real case of "damned if you do, and damned if you don't." I agonized throughout the months I was collecting data and conducting interviews. Eventually, I decided to present myself as one of the veterans of the battle. I asked myself the same sort of questions I asked everyone else, tape-recorded my responses, and then transcribed them.

I remain uncomfortable about describing the deaths of some of the Marines who were killed on Foxtrot Ridge. I certainly don't want to bring additional heartache to the loved ones of those killed by describing the pain these Marines may have suffered. However, I feel it is necessary to describe their deaths in order to describe their courage. Those young men had seen similar dying and suffering among their own friends in the preceding weeks and months, so they knew the risks they faced—yet continued regardless. Also, I don't wish to "soft soap" the horrors of war. I am sure that those killed would be equally keen to show its true horrors so that it would not be "romanticized" and somehow presented as attractive. I apologize for any pain this may cause but feel it is the only true way I can honor those who were killed.

The battle itself was terribly confusing. Most Marines had little or no idea of what was happening elsewhere, even 20 yards to their left or their right. Their battle took place in the "area of responsibility" assigned to them, generally a narrow arc to their immediate front. The noise of the battle was truly ear-shattering. The sky was filled with a multitude of colors:

red tracers, green tracers, colored flares, brilliant flashes of detonating explosions. In the moments of darkness, all eyes strained to see the approaching enemy but then, without notice, they would be blinded by the unexpected flash of an explosion to their front. This situation gave most participants a very restricted view of the action and is reflected over and over again in their recollections. Also, time was of no significance to those participating in the battle. To begin with, the whole sense of "time" is altered in the heightened metabolism of adrenaline coursing through the body. Secondly, everyone was far too busy to be looking at their wristwatches. Because of this, the precise times of the various events is unclear, but probably also unimportant. Because of this inherent confusion of battle, memories and perceptions of the events that took place vary somewhat on some of the minor details (e.g., "Was he carrying an M-14 or an M-16?"). Where this has occurred, I have gone with the "majority opinion" of those interviewed.

I would also like to point out that, while this book is about a *specific* battle, it is also *generally* about the ground war in Vietnam. Most Vietnam veterans, whatever their branch or year of service, will have some similar memories and experiences: their own hellish moments or hours of combat that live with them daily. Many veterans continue to be frustrated by the depiction of the war in the popular media. I hope this book goes some way to telling the truth about the conduct of the war and of those who fought there.

The story is specifically about the battle of Foxtrot Ridge, covering the period from the time when Foxtrot Company climbed up the ridge on May 25, 1968, until they left the ridge 3 days later. I remember Joe Galloway (author of *We Were Soldiers Once . . . And Young**) giving me some sage advice just after my earlier book was published, and I was eagerly awaiting reviews. He warned me about the frustration every author feels when some people criticize "the book you didn't write." These critics may complain "Why didn't you include this? Why didn't you write about that?" In the case of *Foxtrot Ridge*, the "book I didn't write," was the one that gave equal attention to the courage and losses suffered by other Marine units (Echo

---

*Lieutenant General Harold G. Moore U.S.A. (Ret.) and Joseph L. Galloway, *We Were Soldiers Once . . . And Young: Ia Drang, The Battle That Changed the War in Vietnam* (New York: Random House, 1992)

and Golf Companies, 2nd Battalion 3rd Marine Regiment, and India Company, 3rd Battalion 4th Marine Regiment) in subsequent battles on that same ridge. Maybe that one will be written one day too. But this book is primarily about the experiences of the men of Foxtrot Company, 2nd Battalion, 3rd Marines in the initial battle.

In focusing on that narrow time (with the exception of a brief "Epilogue" about those later battles), of necessity, I give only a passing reference to preceding events. One of these preceding events mentioned is that Foxtrot Company's Commanding Officer, Lieutenant Wilbur "Bo" Dishman, left for a 5 day R & R to meet his wife in Hawaii just days before the battle and hence was replaced by another officer, Lieutenant James Jones. What I don't say in the text, but must be acknowledged, is that Lieutenant Dishman had led Foxtrot Company in battle for months. It was very much a product of

Hill 222, where the Marines of Foxtrot 2/3 were sent soon after the battle of Foxtrot Ridge. (Credit: Author's Collection)

his leadership. He had molded it into a fine fighting unit. He had agonized about leaving the unit to go on R & R and had already twice cancelled his plans. The Battalion Commander, Colonel Jack Davis, had ordered Lieutenant Dishman to take the leave and told him that no major combat operations were planned for the next few weeks. So Lieutenant Dishman left and when he arrived back, landing in Da Nang in early June, the whole "rear area" of the 3rd Marine Division was abuzz about the battle that had taken place. Lieutenant Dishman soon learned that it was his unit that they were speaking about. He has kindly spoken with me about this matter and agonizes to this day about the "what-ifs" had he been there. He still reproaches himself for leaving when he did. It is a ghost that still haunts him.

When the battle was over, the Marines were reequipped and rearmed and within days helicoptered to a nearby ridge, known as Hill 222, eerily and ominously similar to the one they had recently left, and where so many of their comrades had died defending it. They would soon be joined there by Lieutenant Dishman and a brand new replacement, 2nd Lieutenant Justin Martin, who would take over command of 2nd Platoon. The final jumping-off point for 2nd Lieutenant Martin's helicopter trip to Hill 222 was Landing Zone (LZ) Hawk, a ramshackle collection of sandbagged bunkers and the site of six artillery pieces, eight mortar tubes and two M-48 tanks that supported the battalion.

Lieutenant Martin arrived at LZ Hawk with the equipment issued him in the rear but which was often inadequate or inappropriate for the bush. An obliging Marine pointed him to a disheveled pile of equipment from which he might salvage an extra canteen and also where he could discard heavy "luxuries" like his gas mask (far better, for the weight, to carry extra ammunition). As he approached the disheveled pile, he realized that this was the equipment of the dead and wounded Marines of the unit that he was soon to join. Each helmet, each cartridge belt, each blood-splattered item represented a dead or wounded Marine.

Lieutenant Justin Martin: I remember vividly coming there to LZ Hawk, seeing those charred packs, the blood-splattered equipment, and then going from that to 222 and looking at the blank, lifeless stares of the guys who were still there. That to me probably made more of an impression on me and bonded me with Fox 2/3 more than any other initial experience I had. For 33 years I've carried a phrase that I think I coined back at that time and I even started to write something about it . . . and I stuck it into my scrapbook and I said, 'Today I realize that Vietnam really is the maddening place.'

The "maddening place" for the handful of U.S. Marines who were there in late May 1968 is undoubtedly the battle of Foxtrot Ridge. For most of them, their memories and recollections of that battle continue to haunt them and guide their lives. Those memories and recollections fill this book.

M.W.W.
Perth, Western Australia
May 28, 2001

FOXTROT RIDGE

A BATTLE REMEMBERED

By mid-May 1968, American ground troops had fought the Vietnam War for seven bloody years. The Communists' Tet Offensive had been soundly defeated some four months previously. With that Offensive, the indigenous Viet Cong also died. The continuing inflow of North Vietnamese Army (NVA) troops at that time was now even more crucial for the Communists' pursuit of the war. The Viet Cong battalions were soon filled with these northern-born conscripts, trained in conventional warfare and unfamiliar with the southern terrain in which they operated. The former guerrilla war essentially ceased.

The huge North Vietnamese Army also continued in its attempts to invade its southern neighbor in its own 10,000-man division-sized units heavily armed with artillery and even tanks. The NVA had the luxury of operating from "neutral" Laos and Cambodia, where they were free from attack. To defend this 800-mile border, the American and South Vietnamese Army established a string of border outposts intended to signal the NVA presence and allow an American counterattack once these NVA troops entered the south. Most American troops were required in the enormous logistic "tail" needed to fight a war 10,000 miles from home. Comparatively few units were available for this mobile mission. These few units were referred to as "maneuver battalions" because they were able to take the war to the enemy.

In May 1968, American casualties were running as high as 500 men killed in action in a week, with a disproportionate number of these casualties coming from the maneuver battalions. These battalions never numbered over 50. Their average field strength was about 500 men in each battalion. Thus, while American peak strength in the war was almost 500,000 troops, the 25,000 men who fought in the maneuver battalions suffered 80% of the casualties.

One such maneuver battalion was the 2nd Battalion, 3rd Marine Regiment. This is the story of one of the battles these men fought: a brief but fierce encounter in May 1968. The story is told by the veterans themselves.

1 | THE MORNING OF MAY 25, 1968

On May 25, 1968, the hundred-or-so Marines of Foxtrot Company walked a short distance down Route 9, the one-lane dirt road that led to Khe Sanh, some 5 miles away. Then they headed off the road into the hilly bush to the south. Although it was only about nine o'clock in the morning, the temperature was already well into the 80s and the air was heavy with humidity. It was the beginning of another sweltering summer day in Vietnam.

Their battalion, the 2nd Battalion, 3rd Marine Regiment (written as 2/3 but spoken as two-three), had acquired the sobriquet of "Rent-a-Battalion." It was not the most glamorous of nicknames but it accurately described their history over the past few months of being temporarily loaned out to whatever unit or location was in the thick of the action and needed help. They'd seen heavy fighting in the Tet Offensive 4 months ago and had been in the bush and in combat, virtually non-stop since then. The battalion, which consisted of Foxtrot and three other 100-man rifle companies (Echo, Golf, and Hotel) had suffered 65 killed and 494 wounded in the past 4 months alone. About one-half of the wounded required only brief hospitalization and were then returned for duty within a few weeks. Even factoring in the wounded returned to duty, the toll on the battalion, and on Foxtrot Company was staggering. So while it was certainly a "blooded and well-oiled machine"(to quote Colonel Jack Davis, the Battalion Commander), it was also both well under strength and continually topped up with new replacements.

For the past 2 months the Marines of Foxtrot Company patrolled the hills on either side of Route 9, climbing up and down these rolling hills during the day, and then digging in at night at constantly changing locations. When it wasn't their turn to stand watch, and if they were lucky enough not to be on a night ambush or patrol, the Marines slept on the rocky ground. If they had the time, they would erect little one-man "hootches" from their waterproof ponchos to protect themselves from the nightly rains. Because they didn't have any home base to return to, they carried everything they owned on their backs or in their pockets. They hadn't had a bath or a shower since just before Operation Pegasus some 8 weeks before. They were tired and dirty, but they knew their job well.

Commanding Foxtrot Company was 1st Lieutenant James L. Jones, a 24-year-old graduate of Georgetown University. Two days before he had been the Executive Officer (second-in-command and referred to as the XO) of Golf Company. He was then advised he'd be temporarily taking over command of Foxtrot Company, thus allowing its "real" Commanding Officer, Lieutenant Wilbur "Bo" Dishman, to get away for some much-needed R & R. Officers, too, had been taking heavy casualties and Lieutenant Jones got the assignment for the simple reason that he was the only available officer.

1st Lieutenant James Jones: I was the XO of Golf Company 2/3 and I was the only Company XO in the battalion, all the other officers having been killed or wounded. It was the only company that had an extra officer. I think Foxtrot Company had Ray Dito. So when my good friend, Bo Dishman, decided to go on R & R, the Battalion Commander, Colonel Davis ('Blackjack' Davis), assigned me temporarily to Foxtrot Company. I'd probably been in the field longer than most other lieutenants in the battalion by that time and I had been in Vietnam since October 1967. I'd gone through seven company commanders who were killed or wounded. So I was temporarily assigned over to Fox Company so Bo could go on R & R.

As luck would have it, no sooner had he taken command of Foxtrot Company than Lieutenant Jones' former unit, Golf

Company, got into a serious firefight. Of its 100-or-so Marines, 15 were killed and 21 wounded, requiring the assistance of Foxtrot.

1st Lieutenant James Jones: When I joined Foxtrot Company, it was in a bivouac site (alongside Route 9). The company was there and my old company, Golf Company, was operating in the area of Foxtrot Ridge but slightly to the west in the high ground. They had just been ambushed. I got a call from Chuck Woodard, who was the company commander of Golf Company. He said, 'Hey, we're really in a trick.' In fact, it was my old platoon that had walked into a U-shaped ambush (North Vietnamese) and they needed some help. So we mounted up the company from that bivouac site and we started up toward the high ground where Golf Company was in its engagement. I elected to try to come at the NVA from a tactical standpoint instead of a frontal charge up the ridgeline by coming at them from the backside. So we headed out in the general direction of Foxtrot Ridge and actually started walking up that ridge but leading toward the firefight.

Also new to Foxtrot Company was Gunnery Sergeant "Gunny" Ralph Larsen. He was replacing Gunnery Sergeant Lawrence Ziegler who, along with four other Foxtrot Marines, had been killed in a brief firefight just 10 days ago on a hilly slope a few miles to the east. Gunny Larsen was new to Foxtrot but certainly not new to the Marines. Thirty-five-year-old Gunny Larsen had joined the Marines on August 4, 1950, at the age of 17. "I convinced my parents I would not go back to school, so they finally signed the papers and let me go." Gunny Larsen was a veteran of many bloody battles against the Communist Chinese while serving with the 5th Marine Regiment in the Korean War.

Gunnery Sergeant Ralph Larsen: I was very new to the company, something like 10 days. It didn't seem that long. I remember the little things even before we started out. Either that day or the day before, we were about to head up the road, get on a truck and go someplace. I remember this kid who was just refusing to get on the truck and go. There was this big hullabaloo and all of a sudden we're ready to go somewhere and he wouldn't get on the truck. Lieutenant Jones called the battalion commander and the colonel said, 'If he don't get on this truck, I want you to shoot him and throw him off in the brush and get on with your mission.' When the kid heard this, he hopped right up on the truck.

In fact, when I joined the company, they were right up the road from LZ Hawk. I got there in the afternoon. I really didn't know what was going on; I just kind of checked the perimeter. It was just kind of a jumping-off place; I guess there wasn't room at Hawk. The next morning, we were going to go hiking up the road and I don't remember where it was now, just sort of a walk in the sun.

Gunny Larsen was extremely fit and of thin, sinewy build. Despite being more than a decade older than most of the Marines of Foxtrot, he had no trouble matching the pace of the company as well as carrying his fair share of ammunition and supplies. But he had a secret he concealed from his young charges. He had sustained a very serious knee injury in a para-chuting accident only 5 years before during a night freefall. He had taken a very hard landing and the resulting injury had placed him on the "temporary disability retired" list. Gunny Larsen wanted to stay in the Marines but was told he would first have to pass a medical examination. He was living in Hawaii at the time and reported to the Army Medical Center there. "I got a physical and they didn't ask me much. They gave me a physical and sent a letter to the Commandant of the Marine Corps saying, 'This guy is all done; he's finished,' or words to that effect." But Gunny Larsen appealed that decision and was ordered to appear before a Medical Board at the Oakland Naval Hospital. "When I got over there, that morning before the Board had even met, I ran into this orthopedic sur-geon I knew at Bethesda Maryland. He says, 'How are you doing?' I says, 'Hey, Good. Want to race up the hill?' Stuff like that. He says, 'Come on. Let me take a look at that knee.' He pulled on and tugged on it and I said, 'Come on. I'm doing fine. I'll give you a demonstration.' That didn't happen but when I went before the Board I found that he was one of the members of the Board. When I went in, people were asking me questions. There were Navy officers and Marine Corps officer representatives and so forth there. They were asking me questions that didn't have anything to do with my condition and finally this Navy captain reaches over across the table and shakes my hand and says, 'Welcome back to the Marine Corps.' What a surprise! That surgeon, he helped me out big time. That got me back in."

Unknown to his young Marines, Gunny Larsen now wore a leg brace concealed under his jungle utility trousers as he climbed the steep slope leading up to what would be known as Foxtrot Ridge.

Gunnery Sergeant Ralph Larsen: Going down the hills was bad news for me. Going up hill no problem. If somebody said, 'Race me,' I'd race them uphill but not downhill.

I do remember us climbing the hill going to the ridge. At the time I didn't know what day it was and it didn't matter. In that situation you don't. But I do remember we were going up there and I was kind of surprised we were going to stay overnight because it was a lousy position. And Lieutenant Jones was too, evidently.

Carrying one of Foxtrot's six M-60 machine guns, Private First Class (PFC) Kevin Henry also struggled up the hill, burdened by his various equipment, food and ammunition, and the 23-pound machine gun—usually referred to, correctly, simply as a "gun." PFC Henry had been in Vietnam since February. A New Jersey native, he had been a student at the University of Colorado but didn't want to return for his sophomore year. So in the summer of 1967, he received his draft notice from the U.S. Army but preempted that service by joining the Marines. "Well there's no way I'm running away to Canada because I wasn't raised that way. And if I'm going, I'm going all the way. I want to be where the action is."

PFC Kevin Henry: It was a very steep climb and it was hot as hell. It was a very inhospitable place. I didn't like being there. Because we were out in the open. And everybody knew that we were there.

Further back in the column and carrying a machine gun

was PFC Robert Croft, born December 20, 1948, in Hixson, Tennessee, about 15 miles north of the Georgia border. Like many of his fellow Marines, his early life had not been easy, but like them, he didn't complain and was thankful for the blessings he did receive. Like so many of his fellow Marines, PFC Croft had grown up around firearms and felt comfortable in their use. "We hunted all our lives, when we were kids, when we were just old enough to carry one. When we were kids we'd lay down in the barn at our grandparents' farm down in Alabama. We stayed down there for awhile 'cause our parents got divorced and all. We'd take a little old .22 and lay up there in the loft for hours at a time; just lay there and shoot gophers getting out in the corn crib. I was about 6 or 7 years old then."

There were several reasons why PFC Croft joined the Marines. One of his best friends had already been killed in Vietnam while serving in the Marines so there were scores to settle. But sibling rivalry probably had as much to do with his decision as anything. "My older brother went in before I did— he went in the Marines. And I always out-bested him, the best I could. In everything, football and everything. So he went in the Marine Corps, I had to go in the Marine Corps. Had to."

He had joined the Marines in 1966 at the age of 17 and was

sent to Guantanamo Bay, Cuba. He had been promoted to Lance Corporal by the time he turned 18 in December 1967 and was ordered to Vietnam. But a last-minute dispute with a disliked sergeant saw him reduced in rank to PFC just prior to leaving Cuba. PFC Croft's easy-going, laconic manner and characteristic regional accent had soon earned him the nickname of "Hillbilly." PFC "Hillbilly" Croft quickly realized his new unit, Foxtrot Company, was a fighting one.

PFC Robert 'Hillbilly' Croft
shoulders his M-60 machine gun.
(Credit: Robert Croft)

PFC Robert "Hillbilly" Croft: See, I hadn't been there long. I got there in March. Actually when I came in, being a new guy and all that, when they brought us out in the choppers—I think there was about five or six of us brought out—then they said, 'We can't set you down right now because your company's under fire,' … and I said, 'Well this is great!'

So they set us down at LZ Hawk or LZ Stud or some- where and we had to wait there. When I first come out, I was a 'a-gunner' (assistant-gunner). The guy who was the gunner, he got wounded or something.

Now on May 25, PFC Croft shouldered his machine gun and climbed up onto the ridge. PFC Croft wasn't displeased by the ridge's location, knowing that its proximity to the road should make resupply easier. Too many times these young Marines had been out of food and water and the expected hel- icopter resupply failed to arrive, sometimes diverted to anoth- er unit, sometimes grounded because of mechanical or weath- er problems.

PFC Robert "Hillbilly" Croft: Well, the weather was pretty fair. We come up. Well, of course we just come off the road up there and went down and set up right there. And I said, 'Well this is pretty good because we're right next to the road and we'll get supplies any- time we want to, you know.' It was just like a big valley and then up on the other side and then there was the road.

PFC Chris Gentry, a tall, thin, very fair-skinned lad moved up the hill carrying an M-16. Nineteen-year-old PFC Gentry was born and raised in Anchorage, Alaska, but was familiar with the hot, humid climate. As a boy, he used to spend sum- mer vacations on his grandfather's farm in Oklahoma. PFC Gentry's grandfather, who had served in both World Wars with the Marines, had given him his first rifle at the age of three. Under his grandfather's close supervision, Chris had used .22 "short" ammunition to shoot grasshoppers off the barbed-wire fence. "That's really where I leaned to shoot."

In many ways, it was not at all surprising that PFC Gentry should find himself, rifle in hand, moving in column up the ridgeline. His grandfather had been a Marine and his father had served as an Army Air Corps pilot in World War II. His uncle was wounded in the Korean War. "In my family it was

important that you go in and serve. It doesn't matter whether it's
2 years or 20 years. Go in, repay some of the obligation that we
should feel for having been part of this country. Do it the best you
can and get it over with."

PFC Chris Gentry: Going up Foxtrot Ridge, we had a heat
casualty. He was in my squad and I told him, 'You don't
understand. Nobody's coming back here. You know you
have to get up and walk.' I can't remember his name. We
got him up to the top of the hill and he was evacuated out.
I remember we left LZ Hawk, walked down the road,
fought our way through the jungle grass, moved up on
top of the hill. We were there several days before the battle.

In command of 1st Platoon was 24-year-old 2nd Lieutenant
Ray Dito. Born and raised in the San Francisco area, Lieutenant
Dito had graduated from San Jose State University. Deferred from
the draft until he graduated, Lieutenant Dito soon received his
notice to report for the induction physical but decided to enlist
ahead of time to get into the officer's program. He had planned to
join the Navy but wound up signing on with the Marines, who
had an office just down the hall from the Navy recruiter. He
reported for duty in April 1967. Soon after arriving in Vietnam in
late 1967, Lieutenant Dito was wounded in action with Foxtrot in
a pitched battle with North Vietnamese regulars during the Tet
Offensive. After several weeks of recuperation from the bullet
wound, he returned to Foxtrot and now found himself climbing
the ridge.

2nd Lieutenant Ray Dito: As part of that activity at that
particular time, we kept working the hills south of
Highway 9. We'd spend some time at LZ Hawk; it seemed
for quite some time. Off and on for weeks it seemed. We
worked a little bit south of the base off of Highway 9 and
then we worked west of the base off of Highway 9, but
generally to the south, once in a while to the north.
We had operated up off that one hill where my platoon
had taken a couple of casualties and Gunny Ziegler was
KIA [Killed In Action]. That hill was east of Foxtrot Ridge,
maybe 5 or 6 kilometers. We had gone back and forth back
into those hills.

2nd Lieutenant Ray Dito in January 1968 with a captured communist 122-mm rocket. (Credit: "Doc" George Riordan, USN, KIA March 10, 1968)

Following a few feet behind Lieutenant Dito was Lance Corporal Jim Chafin, a 19-year-old from Mentor, Ohio. Lance Corporal Chafin was the platoon's radio man and so carried the heavy PRC-25 radio for use by Lieutenant Dito. In addition, he carried a .45 pistol and an M-14 rifle. The M-14 was heavier at 9.1 pounds than the M-16 at 6.1 pounds, and its 7.62-mm ammunition much bulkier than the M-16's smaller 5.56-mm projectile. Lance Corporal Chafin was prepared to carry the extra weight because of the rifle's proven reliability.

Lance Corporal Jim Chafin: I used an M-16 one time and it jammed on me and I said, 'Hell with that. I ain't using that no more.' So I went to an M-14. It was heavier and everything else but, nevertheless, I knew when I pulled that trigger there was something going down range.

Also climbing up toward the crest of the ridge was 21-year-old PFC Dave Kinsella of upstate New York. PFC Kinsella was very unhappy as he struggled uphill, bent forward under the weight of his burden. Although trained as a rifleman, he had been put into the 60-mm mortar squad and now found himself carrying not only his rifle and grenades and other equipment, but also an additional 30 pounds of mortar ammunition.

> **PFC Dave Kinsella:** I can remember going up there [Foxtrot Ridge] and only mainly because I was with mortars at the time and I hadn't been there long. I was the ammo humper. I think I was humping about eight mortar rounds and it was killing me. I think each weighed about four pounds apiece. The other guys carried the base plate, or the tube or certain parts. I can remember humping up onto Foxtrot Ridge. I can remember it was miserably hot because I can remember when we actually got on the hill, just dropping the pack off my back and just stripping it off and complaining about all I wanted to do was go over to the grunts. You know, I was a grunt and I wasn't supposed to be in mortars anyway. I was whining. I can remember saying that to the guys: 'I'm going to the grunts, I'm not going to hump this ammo anymore.' Because it was kicking my butt getting up there.
>
> I don't think it was that far from Route 9 and I think we went on a trail most of the way. Because I remember coming up the end of that ridge that we came up onto the finger of that ridge. We came right up a trail. I don't think anybody was cutting anything.

PFC Kinsella had only been in Vietnam for four weeks, having arrived on April 25, 1968, but had already seen his fair share of action.

> **PFC Dave Kinsella:** When I got there, I remember being at LZ Hawk for a few days, maybe even a little longer than that, I'm not sure. I can remember when we had the firefight about a week or two before. There was about four or five guys who got killed: Diaz, and I forget who all. There was a S-2 [Intelligence] scout. That

was the first guy I ever saw get killed over there. I actually saw him because I was with the mortars and they called us up to the top of that hill. There was a big bomb crater at the top of the hill, and they called us up there. We run up the hill and were setting up the mortar tube inside the bomb crater. He was up on the front edge, shooting down, because it was down into a valley or something. He was shooting down and, all of sudden, he got hit and he just whipped around and he said: 'Oh, my God!' And he just grabbed his chest. Everybody was screaming for a corpsman. The guy was just laid over on his back in the bomb crater and blood was just squirting right out of his chest. It almost looked like he was hit directly through the heart. He was pretty much dead. You know they put a battle dressing on his chest and a battle dressing on his back at the same time but I think he was probably instantly dead after he was hit. And then I remember Gunny Ziegler shortly after that. Being right up beyond the bomb crater, I believe, is where he was—at the top, and got hit. And them taking him down to bottom of the hill because they were bringing in medevac choppers. That was my first, you know, baptism of fire, I guess you would call it.

Near the front of the column and carrying a Stevens 12-gauge pump shotgun was S-2 scout Lance Corporal Robert Kincaid. Born in West Virginia but raised in Ohio, Lance Corporal Kincaid had joined the Marines in July 1967, and arrived in Vietnam on December 5, 1967. Trained as an infantryman, he had first been assigned to the weapons platoon, carrying a machine gun for a few weeks before hearing of a requirement for S-2 scouts. So Lance Corporal Kincaid volunteered and, after a brief course in DaNang, rejoined Foxtrot Company.

Lance Corporal Robert Kincaid: I do remember the hump was hard up the hill and it kicked my butt. I had a 'gook' pack and I had it loaded with everything, extra shotgun shells and frags and all that stuff. I was helping carry some ammo for the machine gun and then I had a claymore mine bag full of shotgun shells. That was the first time I had carried a shotgun to the field and I didn't know or remember how heavy a box of shells was for a shot-gun. I remember it was a difficult hump up the hill. I wasn't walking point but I was pretty close to the point. I remember that the hump up the hill was hard.

Nineteen-year-old San Franciscan Corporal Dave Smith was a forward observer (FO) for the 81-mm mortar platoon located at LZ Hawk, a couple of miles away, back down Route 9. The eight 81-mm mortars of his mortar platoon, heavier (93.5 pounds apiece) and of longer range (4,000 yards maximum range) than the 60-mm mortars (45.2 pounds, 2,000-yard range) which Foxtrot carried with them onto the ridge, provided fire support for all four of the battalion's rifle companies. Corporal Smith, who had been in Vietnam since August 14, 1967, carried a radio that linked him with the mortar platoon. His job was to direct their fire. He was an expert at map-reading and, because the Marines were typically out-numbered and outgunned by the NVA and therefore depend-ent on "supporting arms"—like mortars, artillery and airstrikes—to defeat the enemy, he was fully briefed on the company's plans and movements. He thus had a much better "big picture" view of what was happening.

Corporal Dave Smith on board USS Paul Revere, *off the coast of South Vietnam in October 1967. (Credit: Dave Smith)*

Corporal Dave Smith: We started off back from the LZ a couple days before. We were supposed to go to Hill 1015 across the river. It was a great big, tall hill that was overlooking Khe Sanh. But as we started going out, there was activity farther down Route 9, toward Khe Sanh. So we started moving down that way and we went down the road and then we cut off and went up to what became known as Foxtrot Ridge some two days before the night of the battle.

We were up on Foxtrot Ridge twice, something like a week or ten days before, after Gunny Ziegler got killed. We'd been up there and then moved back off and then back up. I remember I was up there and there was my radio man and myself and a corpsman and one other guy and we didn't have any holes. At least I didn't that night. So the four of us were under a poncho just hugging each other for all we were worth trying to stay warm and dry. I remember we went off of that hill and when we came back I said, 'Shit, we're back up here again.'

2 | THE AFTERNOON AND EVENING OF MAY 25, 1968

The Marines of Foxtrot got to the crest of the ridge but were advised that the enemy had broken contact with Golf Company and there was no longer any need for their assistance. Lieutenant Jones radioed for further orders.

1st Lieutenant James Jones: At that point the North Vietnamese broke contact and we really never had a chance to engage them except we pursued them by harassing fires . . . but it was mostly guesswork. Golf Company withdrew, and we found ourselves at the end of the day on the Ridgeline without any clear orders from the battalion. So I called into the S3 [Operations Section] and I said, 'We're in a reasonably good defensive position.' I recommended we stay here for the evening. And we got the approval to do that.

The Marines established a defensive perimeter near the crest of the ridge. The perimeter thus formed a long, narrow oval, perhaps 100 yards from end to end but only 30 yards across. The extreme eastern edge of the ridgeline overlooked a gradual dip or "saddle," which then rose up to a small bump of ground about 50 yards away, slightly higher than the ridge itself, and thus overlooked it. If the enemy were able to occupy it, they could fire right down at the exposed Marines on the ridge below. Ideally, if they had enough men, the Marines would have stretched their perimeter to encompass that key terrain feature, but they didn't. So they were forced instead to fortify it as a separate position. Manned by a squad or so of Marines, it was occupied day and night. In Marine parlance, this was referred to as an "outpost" or "OP." The Marines quickly dubbed this outpost "the Crow's Nest."

> **1st Lieutenant James Jones:** We looked at the ridgeline and saw what eventually became the Crow's Nest and decided we couldn't leave that undefended because it was high ground, key terrain, overlooking the rest of the position.
>
> At the end of that day, it was a relatively short hike, it wasn't that far, but at the end of the day, we found ourselves there for the evening. We dug in. We heavily reinforced the firepower on the Crow's Nest and the rest from there is history. One of the things that I think is important to note in any recount is that, even though we called ourselves 'a company,' we were scarcely, really, more than almost two reinforced platoons. I remember evacuating, medically, three or four people every day because of dehydration, dysentery or some other sort of medical problem. We were under—if I recall correctly—under 100 in term of total strength.

At the western end of the perimeter the ridge fell away more gradually, the slopes gentler. This northwestern slope was the same avenue Foxtrot Company had used to ascend the ridge earlier that day from Route 9. Additionally, at the extreme western tip, there was a narrow ravine, which dropped away and extended a few hundred yards in the direction of the abandoned Khe Sanh village and Laos beyond it. Further around, on the southwestern slope of the ridge, which faced away from Route 9, a grassy slope dropped gently away to the base of the ridge and a small stand of trees and bushes. Rolling hills and ridges extended into the distance.

The 30 Marines of 1st Platoon, under the command of Lieutenant Dito, were assigned this western end of the ridgeline. They would wrap themselves around that end of the ridge in a series of two-man and three-man fighting positions commonly called "foxholes." Lieutenant Dito would establish his command post (CP) slightly behind 1st Platoon's lines at a location where he could observe and command his Marines.

2nd Lieutenant Ray Dito: At that point I had set up my own little CP, kind of at the base of the arc where we curved around the end of the ridge. That's where I had my radio operator and my bag and I kept my gear there. I let the people know that's where you could find me if you needed me.

Second-in-command to Lieutenant Dito was Platoon Sergeant Joseph Quinn, a tall Pennsylvanian just one month short of his 23rd birthday. With Sergeant Quinn were his three best friends: 22-year-old Corporal Steve Baker, 20-year-old Lance Corporal Michael Smith, and fellow Pennsylvanian, 19-year-old PFC Bill Grist. PFC Grist, who had been in Vietnam for 6 months, had acquired the affectionate nickname, "the Bear," because of his strong physique and his capacity to carry a heavy burden with apparent ease: machine gun ammunition, mortars, claymore.

Sergeant Joseph Quinn: The road [Route 9] was behind us. I remember going up the hill because it was a fairly steep hill going up to the ridge. There was very little foliage on that side of the hill. There were tree lines on the other side.
  Where we came up the hill, that's where 1st Platoon was, maybe a little bit south of there. They wrapped around that end. We had to go out and scout around a little bit and see where likely avenues of approach were, I remember that. I looked over and I said, 'They could come up right up here,' and that's where they put the gun down there. Covering the tree line. Because they could sneak up right there. That's why we put the gun down there.

The remaining Marines of 2nd and 3rd Platoons formed the rest of the perimeter, circling the ridge just below its crest in a series of foxholes spaced about 20 yards apart. Second Platoon was assigned the eastern end of the ridge, facing the saddle and the Crow's Nest beyond with 3rd Platoon completing the link back with Lieutenant Dito's men. The Crow's Nest formed its own separate perimeter some 50 yards to the east of the ridge itself.
  As dusk approached, the Marines settled into their stan-

dard night time defensive routines. Most foxholes were manned by three Marines, and the three took turns standing watch in their defensive positions. Generally, the Marines did 90-minute watches, commencing just before dark and ending at first light when they would usually "saddle up" in preparation for moving. So, the first Marine would stand watch from 9:00 PM to 10:30 PM, while the other two lay sleeping on the ground nearby. At 10:30 PM, he would awaken the next Marine for his 90-minute shift and then lie down on the ground nearby to sleep, to be awakened 3 hours later for his second turn (1:30 AM to 3:00 AM). This broken sleeping pattern added to the Marines' general fatigue but was deemed a better alternative than solid, 3-hour shifts, which risked Marines losing concentration and even falling asleep while on guard. So, all the positions on the ridge were manned throughout the night and those Marines asleep were only an arm's length away.

3 | MAY 26, 1968

The night of May 25 was uneventful. Instead of "saddling up" and moving the next morning, the Marines of Foxtrot Company were surprised to discover they were to remain on the ridge. Usually they moved every day, both in order to aggressively search for the enemy but also, defensively, to be a more difficult target for the NVA. Despite their concerns, most of the Marines were happy enough that they didn't have to again shoulder their heavy burdens and climb up and down these familiar hills yet again in the blistering heat. When they realized they would spend a second night on the ridge, they attempted to improve their shallow foxholes, often with little success because of the rock-hard soil. Every third or fourth Marine carried a small folding shovel, called an entrenching tool (or just "E tool"), with which to scrape out a hole, but these tools were predictably inadequate for this engineering challenge. The Marines did the best they could, but in some parts of the perimeter, where the ground was hardest, these holes were only perhaps 18 inches deep. With a unit so seriously understrength, there was little tactical option. They could only dig in and wait.

1st Lieutenant James Jones: There was no question that we were not going to patrol far from the perimeter with that kind of strength. We either had to all go or nobody go. So we essentially thought Khe Sanh was obviously the area that was getting the most attention. For a couple of days we sort of satisfied ourselves with waiting for the battalion to tell us what they wanted us to do

next and observing the terrain between us and the
Laotian border, featuring the prominent key terrain of
Co Roc where the North Vietnamese artillery was
reportedly dug in, in bunkers, caves and the like.

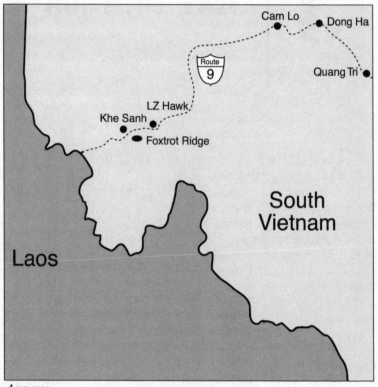

Area map

Foxtrot Ridge soon established itself as an ideal vantage
point. Because of the meandering border, Laotian territory lay
a few miles to the west (past the abandoned Khe Sanh village)
and also to the south. Foxtrot Ridge and its 100 Marines were
thus the most extreme American or Allied position. There was
no one else between them and the Laotian border, and the estimated 20,000 NVA troops sheltering there close by.

A particularly effective vantage point was provided by the
Crow's Nest and its rotating complement of Marines. It was
manned day and night. The job was taken in turn from men
drawn from the various platoons. One Marine, though, was a
"constant" in its manning: artillery forward observer (FO),

PFC Harold Blunk of Chicago. Officially, PFC Blunk didn't "belong" to Foxtrot; he was actually a part of the battalion's artillery battery (Bravo Battery, 1st Battalion, 12th Marine Regiment) whose six 105-mm howitzers fired in support of Foxtrot and the three other rifle companies. These weapons, with a range of over 11,000 meters, were located at nearby Landing Zone (LZ) Hawk. PFC Blunk's radio was normally tuned to a frequency used by the artillery battery. He could thus liaise with them and coordinate their fire.

> **PFC Harold Blunk:** What I recall was being down at the CP with Fox company. They had—not banished—but certainly said that, 'You're the forward observer and the best observation point is from the Crow's Nest.' I went up the Crow's Nest and that's where I stayed. I lived up there for the three days we were on that hill and tried to improve the position up there and had patrols walking through me. I don't even recall going down to get food, C rations, when the resupply came in. I basically slept and stayed up there all day. My mission up there was to call in fire missions out into the valley.

PFC Harold Blunk (left) and an unidentified Marine with binoculars scanning the hills to the south. The Crow's Nest, May 27, 1968. (Credit: Harold Blunk).

Even though PFC Blunk had just turned 21 the month before and even though he was just a PFC, most Marines in Foxtrot assumed he was both older and more senior. Many of them assumed he was an officer. PFC Blunk's childhood had forced him to grow up quickly. His father had died when he was only 5 years old. "It was a trucking accident and they brought home this crushed suitcase of his and a bloody watch." PFC Blunk was suddenly forced to become the man of the family. His memories of childhood were that, while other kids were playing basketball or doing activities at school, he was out working or helping his mother. It forced him to mature quickly. His job in Vietnam required every ounce of this maturity.

PFC Harold Blunk: My position, being a PFC, being school-trained as an FO at Camp Pendleton and then being able to call in artillery and sent into the field, is probably one of the most unusual, responsible positions. Being in on what was happening meant that other people would come up to me and ask what was happening. I certainly had to have the ear of the company commander to know where we were going, what our objective was. The rest of the company was never privy to any of that kind of information. I was on the radio with people to know what was going on because I had to call in fire missions and be aware of the terrain and which direction we were going in order to plan fire missions. I was more like a gypsy and didn't get to be with anybody other than a radio operator here and there.

PFC Blunk was thus an "attachment" to Foxtrot Company, but Bravo Battery was responsible for his administrative matters. Gunnery Sergeant Larsen learned to have special respect for PFC Blunk and noted that Bravo Battery didn't "treat him well," especially in the way of promotions and other forms of recognition.

Gunnery Sergeant Ralph Larsen: Harold Blunk, he impressed me right from the 'get go.' He was with Fox even afterward and that's when I got to know him. His people [the artillery battery] never took care of him.

PFC Blunk spent his days up on the Crow's Nest peering

into the distance with binoculars. He had an ideal vantage point from which to observe into Laos and sight NVA movements from their sheltered bases there. At 5:30 PM on May 26, he observed a column of six NVA soldiers, wearing Soviet-style steel helmets and carrying packs and rifles, moving through the waist-high grass in the distance. He quickly called in artillery, the soldiers disappearing in the impacting rounds. At 7:05 PM he spotted another column. Again the NVA were wearing helmets and carrying rifles and packs. This time his artillery mission was followed up by an airstrike from two F4 Phantom jets. A spotter plane confirmed not only dead NVA soldiers, but also 15 fresh bunkers, indicating the enemy was there in strength.

The Crow's Nest was proving a valuable piece of real estate for the Marines and was clearly making life difficult for the NVA. Despite their concerns about remaining in the same place, the Marines of Foxtrot were advised by their Battalion Commander, Colonel Jack Davis, that they would spend a second night on the ridge and continue to observe enemy movement. The men of Foxtrot prepared for the second night on the ridge and again organized and manned their defenses.

There was a brief flurry of commotion in the middle of the night when an observant Marine on the southern slope spotted NVA soldiers several hundred yards off in the distance near Laos. The Marine was using the newly invented "starlight," night vision scope. It was big, awkward, and quickly drained its batteries, but it was a godsend to the Marines, who otherwise would not have seen the distant movement. The NVA soldiers posed no threat to Foxtrot Company; they were simply passing by across their front, headed off to some unknown objective closer to Khe Sanh. But Corporal Smith, the 81-mm mortar FO, double-checked through the starlight scope and then radioed back to LZ Hawk to order a barrage of deadly mortars to rain down upon the unsuspecting NVA. Most of the Marines of Foxtrot remained unaware of this and assumed it was routine harassment and interdiction fire, random barrages of fire sometimes directed onto likely approaches or enemy locations. Those Marines not on watch simply slept through it unaware. Despite the brief activity in the distance, the night of May 26 passed quietly and uneventfully for the Marines of Foxtrot Company.

THE MORNING OF MAY 27, 1968

As dawn broke on the morning of May 27, after two nights on the ridge, Lieutenant Jones continued to be concerned about the possibility of enemy attack and the capability of his defenses. His defense of the ridge consisted of two separate perimeters: the smaller squad-sized one on the Crow's Nest and the main one around the crest of the ridge itself. In this main perimeter, there were four sectors: the western finger (those positions that wrapped around that end of the ridge and

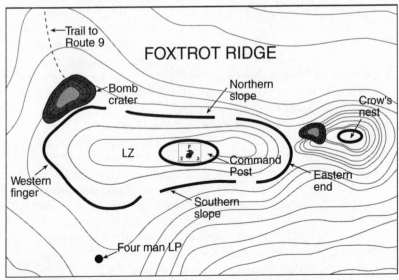

Foxtrot Ridge

overlooked the gentler grassy slopes and the trail Foxtrot had used to climb up), the northern slope of the ridge (facing Route 9), the eastern end of the ridge (facing the Crow's Nest), and the southern slope (facing away from Route 9).

In the middle of the ridge—still only a stone's throw from the Marines on the northern and southern slopes—Lieutenant Jones had established his command post, which consisted of himself, his radio operator, Gunny Larsen, Corporal Smith and a few others.

THE COMMAND POST

Lieutenant Jones realized that Foxtrot was seriously impeding the NVA's ability to move troops in the vicinity and had become a real thorn in their side. NVA heavy artillery, huge Soviet 152-mm field guns, firing from nearby Co Roc mountain in Laos, tried lobbing shells onto the Marines' positions but were unable to score hits. It became clear that the NVA would need to take action and remove the Marines of Foxtrot Company from their vantage point on the ridge.

1st Lieutenant James Jones: For about 24 hours nothing much happened. And then we started occasionally sighting in on targets of opportunity at great distances. We noticed constant movement. As it turns out, in retrospect, we were sitting astride a major infiltration route. Ultimately, Co Roc did try to range us a few times but by virtue of the angle of the ridge, they either shot short or long but they never could hit it with their artillery. And I think, putting myself in the North Vietnamese minds, our presence there was just not acceptable. We were shooting a lot of artillery. We constantly had long-range vision out, and every time we saw something, we just fired. And so, because they couldn't drive us off with artillery, I think they somewhere made the decision that this was intolerable. And I remember the afternoon of the battle. I remember an intelligence report which we routinely assessed but generally disregarded because they were notoriously inaccurate. But I remember being called by the battalion saying, 'Sensors have picked up large movement about 4,000 meters south of your position, toward the border.' I remember taking it seriously enough to make sure that that evening we really did put as much firepower as we could up on the Crow's Nest. I think we put twice as many people as a matter of fact. We talked about it at the platoon commanders' meeting that night before we sent out the listening posts and we made sure that we called in artillery, prepositioned the defensive fires and also 81s, M-60s as we normally did, 360 degrees around the perimeter. That's essentially the situation as I recall.

Lieutenant Jones, just like every other Marine of Foxtrot Company, felt very uncomfortable about remaining in the exposed position for so many consecutive days. Each day that they remained, he constantly passed these concerns along to the battalion headquarters and sought permission to move Foxtrot Company to a different location. Eventually the Battalion Commander, suffering from a then not-yet-diagnosed brain aneurysm, grew tired of Lieutenant Jones' constant requests.

1st Lieutenant James Jones: I remember one time the day before the battle inquiring of the battalion what their plans were because I was uncomfortable sitting there for more than a day. My own preferred technique was to sit tight if you're going to during the day and then move at night because then you can move out under the cover of darkness.

I wanted to leave but evidently we were getting some pretty good results with the artillery, and the battalion commander, matter of fact, got tired of my asking the question and got on the hook (on the phone) personally and gave me an ass-chewing and said, 'I'll tell you when to move!' If you talk to other people, who were closer to him in the battalion, they would tell you that he had some very, very violent mood swings. He was probably under some pretty intense pain from headaches and things like that, without knowing what it actually was. I'll never forget the tongue-lashing I got for being insistent that we move. These mood swings would come just as quickly as they'd disappear, also. So anyway, we were where

we were and those were the major events leading up
to the evening in question.

Corporal Smith was within easy earshot of Lieutenant
Jones. He had dug a hole about 20 yards further to the west.

Corporal Dave Smith: I was just to the west of the CP
group. I started off by the CP group in the middle of the
hill, kind of closer to 1st Platoon. I was between Jones
and Larsen and Dito and the 1st Platoon CP. I was in a
hole with my radio man. He'd only been with me for
something like four days. Also included in there was the
other artillery officer FO whose name was Heinz.

In the same general vicinity was Gunny Larsen, the senior
enlisted Marine in the company. Like just about every other
Marine in Foxtrot, he wasn't happy about remaining there yet
another night.

Gunnery Sergeant Ralph Larsen: I was to the west of
this little CP perimeter. Right next to me was Lieutenant
Heinz [the senior artillery observer who stayed in the
main perimeter]. He was elevated a little bit. And then I
guess Lieutenant Jones was next to him, his radio man
and so forth.

It was an odd position. It was a rotten place to stay. It
was a bad place for a defensive position. Of course, we
didn't have many people. They did know there were
'Indians' out there and the 'Indians,' when they found
out we were there, said, 'Hey, here we go. We got us a
target.'

THE CROW'S NEST

At the Crow's Nest, PFC Blunk continued to observe the
hills in the distance through his binoculars. One group of ten to
twelve Marines would climb the trail leading from the ridge
below and stay throughout the day. As darkness approached, a
different group of Marines, again selected from the various
platoons from the company below, would relieve them and
take up position for the night. The other Marines would thus

rotate through on a continuing basis while PFC Blunk remained throughout. In the process he got to know most of the Marines of Foxtrot briefly, but never formed deeper bonds or friendships. This was typical of his role as an "attached" forward observer.

PFC Harold Blunk: When I call myself a gypsy—that was my life in Vietnam. I went to other companies. At Foxtrot Ridge they would send a gun team or whatever up there during the day and then they would rotate them and send up another team at night and another team during the day. Consequently, people would have to hump that considerably steep hill there and, of course my being up there, I wasn't asked to go back to the company position too often plus I was ordered to go up there. So I would just go up there—I had a pair of binoculars—and I would orientate myself up there and look out at the hills and valleys. I would call in fire missions that were in different approach areas that would look like suspected targets . . . and direct that fire into that valley and get it right on target.

Joining PFC Blunk in the Crow's Nest was a new arrival to Foxtrot: another "attachment," Corporal Kevin Howell. Corporal Howell was a Canadian citizen and a veteran of 4 years in the Canadian Air Force's Military Police. On the day of his honorable discharge from the Canadian forces, he had driven south to New York and fulfilled his childhood ambition of joining the U.S. Marines. But before doing so, he extracted a guarantee from the Marine recruiter: he was promised he would be assigned to a combat unit and guaranteed to go to Vietnam. While many Marines joked about the false promises given by recruiters, it appears this time the recruiters were true to their word.

Corporal Kevin "Canadian" Howell: I was in 3rd Force Recon as a sniper. The rear for me was Quang Tri, with 3rd Force. I had been out for about two weeks, and I'd been back about three days. Major Paddy Collins was my CO and he came in and he told us what was going on. We were told that a company that was down to half strength because of attrition and wounds and disease

and stuff like that. They had settled in on a hill, kind of
like resupplying and stuff like that. The CO had gone
on R & R and they were trying to get support out there
when they noticed that they were running into constant
contact. The Gunny had estimated the possibility of
3,000 enemy surrounding the hill. I thought, back in the
rear when I'm getting this info, that everybody out
there had it. But they didn't. In Recon there's always a
little bit more word put out than with the regular line
units. I heard that about ten o'clock in the morning, and
about noon or so, I was down in the LZ and got chop-
pered in.

That's the first time I had saw Lieutenant Jones. I had
just come in and he was sitting on a crate and all he had
on was a pair of shorts and boots, and a hat. He said,
'We want you on that position over there. It's an
OP/LP. I wish we had more people but we only have a
handful of people to man it.' And it was called the
Crow's Nest. That's where I met Hillbilly and 'Mouse'
Espejo. A great guy. Anyway, they were the machine
gun team out there.

THE WESTERN FINGER

The western finger encompassed the most gradual slopes
of the ridge and therefore the easiest access. Foxtrot Company
itself had chosen that avenue to climb the ridge.

2nd Lieutenant Ray Dito: I can vaguely remember
trekking up there from Highway 9. It didn't appear
very difficult to get there. Up and down a little bit but,
compared to some of the other hills we had humped,
this was not that bad. The north side of Foxtrot Ridge,
the side we accessed from Highway 9, had almost like
little tiers getting up to the crest of the hill. From the
ravine you rock up a little rise and then you'd walk
along the flat and up a little bit higher and then up a little bit higher. It wasn't real steep or difficult.

Lieutenant Dito's 1st Platoon was assigned this western
finger of the ridge. There was also a small flat area that was

used as a helicopter landing zone for resupply. He surveyed the area assigned to him, assessed its likely avenues of approach, and planned his defense against possible attack.

2nd Lieutenant Ray Dito: I took the entire northwestern part of the whole ridge. We covered the end, the western side, the northwestern tip and then down on the southwestern side where we linked up with the other platoon. It was most of the LZ area, and that area that stretched out a little to the west, toward Laos.

Off that finger there was a deep ravine that ran west and I figured that was a likely avenue of approach in addition to the tree line to the south. They could get well to our north by coming up that ravine. So in my mind I figured, well, we have this tree line that has a gradual slope coming up to our position, so that's where the listening post was going to be. It was our most vulnerable position. We wanted somebody out in front there, so I had that manned. We'd have positions on the perimeter behind there, and then there's this ravine. I felt this would be another avenue of approach where they could come around behind us. I figured if they didn't come up through the listening post, then the most likely avenue was the ravine. So I figure I'm going to initially bring some fire to bear there. I felt the mortars would do a good job of breaking up any groups that tried to come in through there. This was part of my plan for the night. At first indication of any movement down there, I was going to use the mortars, no matter what.

One of the three ten-man squads in Lieutenant Dito's platoon was commanded by Corporal Ron Lockley of Houston, Texas. He had acquired the nickname of "Pappy" as a consequence of celebrating his 24th birthday while in boot camp. He had been in Vietnam since January 1968.

Corporal Ron "Pappy" Lockley: I had an M-16. I'd been carrying the M-14 and I don't know but there was this Marine. He was a little, short, heavy-set guy. For some reason me and him had traded rifles. So I had the M-16 and he had the M-14 and he ended up that night on the Crow's Nest.

To the right of Corporal Lockley was 22-year-old Lance Corporal Moses Bacote, a machine gunner from St. Petersburg, Florida. Lance Corporal Randy Huber, a 19-year-old Pennsylvanian, was there, too.

Corporal Ron "Pappy" Lockley: I would have been on the northwest corner. The next position over on my right was our machine gunner, a guy named Moses. I don't remember, but Randy Huber might have been with him in that machine gun position. He was probably the guy over there that I was attached to the most, Randy Huber. He was like a kid brother to me. Me and him were inseparable. If it was his turn to walk point, I walked with him.

Corporal Lockley's squad, which included Lance Corporal Bacote's machine gun, overlooked an area in which there was a large bomb crater. From its massive size it was probably the result of a previous B-52 "arc light" bombing mission. The problem was that the bomb crater was just a few feet in front of the machine gun position and beyond its outer lip. About 20 yards away, the terrain dropped away and so the Marines were "blind" to approach from that area. Ideally, of course, the perimeter would have stretched around the outside of the crater and encompassed it, but the Marines of Foxtrot lacked the manpower for that larger perimeter. Corporal Lockley took his concerns to Lieutenant Dito.

Corporal Ron "Pappy" Lockley: Right in front of that machine gun position was a bomb crater and you couldn't see right over the outside edge of that bomb crater. The edge of the bomb crater was 10 foot in front of the machine gun position. Then you had the expanse of the bomb crater and then it dropped off the other side, so the bomb crater was—what? I don't remember exactly how big they were. I was really concerned about that, especially us staying there day after day. So I remember going to the CO and telling him, 'Hey, it's not a real good setup here because we can't see over that thing.'

To the left of Corporal Lockley, Corporal Baker's squad prepared their defenses on the westernmost tip of the ridge.

Knowing they would spend another night there, the Marines continued to scrape at the hard soil, inching their foxholes deeper. The Marines of Foxtrot were quite happy despite their concerns about staying on the ridge. A resupply helicopter had arrived around midday, bringing several crates of C rations as well as water and, most importantly, mail. Especially elated was 20-year-old Lance Corporal Michael Smith. "Smitty," who had joined the Marines in Bedford, Indiana, and arrived in Vietnam a few days before Christmas 1967, received a letter and photos from his wife. Lance Corporal Smith "whooped" and hollered as he read the news of his newborn child and proudly showed the photos to all his friends in Foxtrot. PFC Bill, "the Bear," Grist slapped his good friend on the back and embraced him in congratulations. Platoon Sergeant Joe Quinn, too, shook Smitty's hand and smiled broadly in their shared joy.

But Sergeant Quinn was suddenly approached by Lieutenant Dito and told he was being reassigned for the next day or two. The Platoon Commander for 2nd Platoon, the 30 or so Marines at the opposite end of the ridge facing the Crow's Nest, had been medevacced out on the resupply helicopter. Sergeant Quinn was ordered to fill in for him and take command of 2nd Platoon. So Sergeant Quinn shrugged and said goodbye to his friends before dutifully walking the hundred yards or so to the other end of the perimeter and assuming his new responsibilities.

Sergeant Joseph Quinn: I was with Grist and those guys on the west side of the hill. The reason I was over in 2nd Platoon's area that night was—I was a sergeant then—they told me that one of the lieutenants got malaria or something and he had to be medevacced out. He was removed so they put me as the platoon commander. That was the day before the actual battle. That's how I got to the other end. That's why I didn't know anybody over there. I mean, I knew them to see them but I don't remember who they were. I remember the squad that I was in.

Bill Grist, the whole time I was over there, I was only separated for that one day. I was in the hole with him because he was my radio man on the other end. I was a platoon sergeant. Our hole was somewhere in the middle. We would have had guys on both sides of us near

the middle of 1st Platoon pretty much at the extreme
end of the finger. That's where Bill Grist was. He was a
radio man and then he carried an M-79. His nickname
was 'the Bear' because he'd carry all kinds of stuff. Real
well-built kid, strong. He was a PFC.

We had a pact, if I got killed, he'd visit my mother and
vice-versa. Smitty, he had black curly hair. He was just
recently married and when he was over there his wife
had the baby and he was passing the picture around.
Baker was a squad leader.

Lance Corporal Alan Walker was the squad leader for one
of Foxtrot's two 60-mm mortar teams and his position was two
or three foxholes to the left of PFC Grist, Corporal Baker, and
Lance Corporal Smith. Lance Corporal Walker's mortar position faced southward and looked down the grassy slope onto
the tree line some 50 yards below them. Lance Corporal Walker
was a Native American, a member of the Winnebago tribe with
strong warrior traditions from Nebraska. His great-grandfa-
ther, William Hatchett, had earned great distinction fighting
alongside Chief Little Priest in the 1860s. With no disrespect
intended, Lance Corporal Walker soon acquired the nickname
of "Chief" by his fellow Marines. While it was unusual for
mortars to be on line (usually they would be located inside the
lines near the command post), the narrow perimeter precluded
any real inside-the-lines area. Also, Foxtrot was so seriously
understrength that their extra manpower was required on its
overstretched defenses. While Lance Corporal Walker was the
mortar's gunner and only carried a .45 pistol, the other three
members of his squad carried M-16s and so their firepower
was required on the company's perimeter defenses.

Lance Corporal Alan "Chief" Walker: We had been
there one time before. And we set up. You know that
was a mortar pit, believe it or not. Whoever had been
up there prior to us dug that out as a mortar pit. So, we
just went back over there and set up. It's kind of unusual to have a mortar on line because we don't carry
enough bullets to sustain a fight. And where we was, it
was really a gentle slope.

Also in the mortar team was PFC Kinsella. Immediately to

Lance Corporal Alan "Chief" Walker (Credit: Alan Walker)

their right was the 3.5-inch rocket launcher team, usually referred to simply as "rockets," and to their left was a machine gun team.

PFC Dave Kinsella: We were actually in a hole on the line which was unusual, too. We were usually inside the lines. It almost seems to me that on my right was the rockets, going towards the point, going towards the finger of the ridge, towards 1st Platoon. On the right was rockets and, on the left, it almost seems to me there was a machine gun over there somewhere but I'm not sure if it was right next to us. I don't think they would have had three weapons set up right next to each other. But I'm almost positive that the rockets were to the right.

The 3.5-inch rocket launcher team consisted of 21-year-old Lance Corporal Ralph Luebers, PFC Reuben Jacabo, and another Marine. Lance Corporal Luebers was armed with the 3.5-inch launcher and carried a .45 pistol for personal defense. The two other Marines in his team were armed with M-16s and, in addition to their rifles and ammunition, each carried two 9-pound rockets for the launcher.

THE SOUTHERN SLOPE (away from Route 9)

A short distance to the left, and facing due south, PFC Dale Braden, 4 months shy of his 19th birthday, surveyed the foxhole to which he was assigned. PFC Braden, of Poplar Bluff, Missouri, had joined the Marines while still in his senior year of high school. He had joined along with several friends, in what the Marine Corps called its "Buddy Plan." This allowed a group of friends to sign up together several weeks before they graduated, deferring their actual start date until graduation, at which time they would all report and train together. However, when PFC Braden and his friends reported to the St. Louis Induction Center as planned, he discovered that there was some mistake in his paperwork and he was sent back home while his friends boarded busses headed for the Marine Corps Recruit Depot, Parris Island. His paperwork was sorted out within a couple of weeks but, because of the delay, he was assigned to a later-starting platoon and would never train or serve alongside his high school friends as promised. "So much for the Buddy Plan," he mused.

PFC Braden had been in Vietnam since April but had just rejoined the company that afternoon, having flown in on the resupply helicopter along with Corporal Howell. PFC Braden had been in the rear at Quang Tri, being fitted with new eyeglasses.

PFC Dale Braden: I wasn't with the rest of the guys when they went up there. I was back in the rear getting glasses. What I did, I was down at LZ Hawk and the chopper came to take mail and resupply up to the ridge. I just got with the company that afternoon. See, I had just come up.

Further to the left, and also facing due south, Lance Corporal Steve Mylin prepared for that third night on the ridge. Lance

Corporal Mylin of Lancaster, Pennsylvania, had been in Vietnam for 9 months and knew the enemy well.

Lance Corporal Steve Mylin: We had been up in that area. We were running patrols. We were up in those hills for a couple of days and we would change positions every day. On Foxtrot Ridge we spent two days there. We would never set in on the same hill two nights in a row. And they said, 'Improve your fighting holes because we're going to stay another night.' We would usually just dig a half-assed fighting hole. I can remember the second day they said, 'We're staying here tonight,' and that's what saved our life. There was a broken-down piece of tree—a log—out in front of our position, and I can remember the three of us drug that back and placed that in front of our hole.

Lance Corporal Robert Kinkaid, the S-2 scout, started out with the command post group in the middle of the perimeter but soon found himself assigned to the perimeter defenses. He quickly latched on to an old friend from his former days as a machine gunner.

Lance Corporal Robert Kincaid: I was with the head-quarters group. That's where I started from. But then when we set in for the night position, they had more than enough to stand the watches there at the company with Jones. So I just went over to 3rd Platoon and plopped in with Charlie Kohler on his position where he had the machine gun.

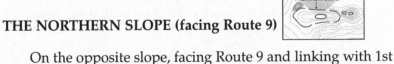

THE NORTHERN SLOPE (facing Route 9)

On the opposite slope, facing Route 9 and linking with 1st Platoon, which wrapped around the finger to their left, the Marines had the advantage of a steeper gradient leading up to them. This would make it more difficult for the enemy to approach quickly or stealthfully. One of the Marines there was 21-year-old Sergeant Dave McCoy. Born in Windsor, England, Sergeant McCoy was raised in Ypsilanti, Michigan, where he joined the Marines in July 1965. This was Sergeant McCoy's second tour of Vietnam. He had previously served with the 3rd Battalion, 4th Marines, and had seen heavy fighting in Operations Prairie and Hastings.

Marine foxhole on northern slope of Foxtrot Ridge. Note captured ChiCom grenades and AK-47. (Credit: Louis Lopez)

Sergeant Dave McCoy: We knew they were all over the place there. I started bitching from day one that we'd been there too long. After the first night I told them we'd been there too long. Let's get out of here. I didn't like the situation. I didn't like all the movement we were seeing around us. I didn't like any of that because I'd seen it all before.

Two of the 30 or so Marines in Sergeant McCoy's platoon were Chicagoan Lance Corporal Fercin "Chico" Rodriquez and Corporal Gary "Tex" La Bonte of Mesquite, Texas.

Sergeant Dave McCoy: Chico was three holes back from the 1st Platoon lines where it started to horseshoe on the south side to turn around to the north. He was the third position in. And La Bonte was closer to 3rd

Platoon's position where they tied in on the north side of their horseshoe. He was about two or three holes away from the tie in of that point.

Sergeant Hubert Pressler, known as "Dick" to his friends, was Weapons Platoon Commander but most of his men—the machine gunners and rocket teams—had been assigned to the various other platoons. So he found himself primarily involved with the 60-mm mortar which was set up near Lieutenant Jones' command post. Twenty-five-year-old Sergeant Pressler from Elkhart, Indiana, had been in Vietnam only one month but was an experienced Marine, having joined in 1961. Sergeant Pressler took up a position along the northern perimeter.

Sergeant Hubert "Dick" Pressler: I was in a foxhole facing the road on that side a little bit toward the west. The Crow's Nest was basically over my right shoulder, back. And on the top of that hill, right there, on the top I had a mortar tube—a 60 mike-mike—sitting up there.

In the morning and early afternoon of May 27, PFC Croft was also assigned to a position on the northern perimeter facing Route 9. Having spent two nights there already, he and his assistant gunner had laboriously dug a deep foxhole. But on the afternoon of May 27, he was advised that it was his machine gun team's turn to spend a night up on the Crow's Nest.

PFC Robert "Hillbilly" Croft: As far as I can tell I was with 2nd Platoon because I was on the road side, the side that the road was on. My a-gunner, his nickname was 'Mouse,' Julio Espejo, he was a little bitty dark-skinned guy. He was my a-gunner. We dug a great hole over there you know. See, they took turns of putting us up there [on the Crow's Nest]. And of course Blunk, he was up there. In the evening it was me and my a-gunner's time to go up there. When we got up there, well it was in the evening when they sent us up there. They said, 'Well, it's your time to go up there and relieve those guys.'

So PFC Croft and PFC Espejo gathered up their weapons and ammunition and prepared to take their turn up on the Crow's Nest.

THE EASTERN END (facing the Crow's Nest)

At the eastern end of the perimeter, looking directly out across the saddle to the Crow's Nest beyond, PFC Mark Woodruff readied himself for the third night on the ridge. PFC Woodruff, had completed two years at El Camino Junior College in California before enlisting in the Marines. PFC Woodruff carried a 3.5-inch rocket launcher and, despite everyone's joking reference to it as being a Korean War antique, he liked it. He knew it was the most powerful direct-fire weapon available to the company in those first moments of combat before artillery or mortars or air support could arrive. Although he had to admit it was probably just a "lucky shot," the launcher had proven its worth when, just 10 days ago, the day before his 21st birthday, he had managed to put a 9-pound antitank round right into the gunslit of an NVA bunker, destroying it and killing the three NVA soldiers who had moments before killed Gunny Ziegler and the S-2 scout.

> **PFC Mark Woodruff:** I had a pretty good field of fire in front of me. There'd been a grass fire earlier in the day. I'm not sure how it got started, maybe a trip flare went off and started it. Anyway, I could see pretty clearly to my front because the grass had burned off. It was just a kind of gentle slope dropping off to that saddle area, maybe a drop of a few feet before rising up to where the Crow's Nest was, maybe 60 or so yards away. There was an old bomb crater—those hills around Khe Sanh were just pock-marked with craters—out in front of me, maybe a little to my left. It was about two-thirds the way to the Crow's Nest. I remember making a mental note about where it was because I knew we'd need to keep an eye on that at night.

PFC Kevin Henry also faced the saddle in a machine gun position just to the right of PFC Woodruff, some 20 yards away.

PFC Mark Woodruff, armed with a 3.5" rocket launcher, at LZ Hawk in early May 1968. (Credit: Author's collection)

PFC Kevin Henry: We were sitting on the ground overlooking the saddle. The reason we put the gun there, or the reason Jones told me to put the gun there—I'm not really sure who made the decision—was because it was a very good field of fire. And that's why Woodruff had the rocket there, also. We didn't have to clear a field of fire because, if we had to fire, we'd be firing down on somebody.

Lance Corporal Doug "Deuce" Near was the squad leader for rockets although his squad now numbered only three men, including PFC Woodruff. Lance Corporal Near was well aware of the dangers present and worked along with the others to scrape their holes deeper. Even so, neither of the two holes was more than 2 feet deep.

Lance Corporal Doug "Deuce" Near: The ground. It was just hard rock. It seemed the ground just wouldn't break. But somehow we managed.

Alaskan PFC Gentry was located in that same area, slightly further around to the right.

PFC Chris Gentry: My normal position would have been facing that Crow's Nest. I was in a foxhole right on the edge of the trail going up to the Crow's Nest. It was right on the left-hand side of the trail. Someone was cooking some chow and set the grass on fire. We fought that grass fire for about an hour, maybe. I mean it burned a lot of the terrain. I wrote a letter to my parents saying, 'I have been in the biggest firefight of my time in Vietnam,' and then went on to tell that the hill caught on fire and we were battling the grassfire.

PFC Gentry placed the letter to his parents in the nylon mailbag that lay in the tall grass on the LZ near the other end of the ridge. This was the same mailbag that had been used earlier in the day to bring out the letter from Lance Corporal Smith's wife. It would be picked up and taken to the rear by the next resupply helicopter.

Soon after arriving back from the short walk to the LZ, PFC Gentry was advised that he would not be remaining in that position that night. Instead, it was his turn to join a dozen other Marines manning the Crow's Nest. When PFC Gentry got tapped on the shoulder to go, his good friend 18-year-old PFC Lawrence Arthur quickly volunteered to go too.

PFC Chris Gentry: Larry and I were in the same foxhole and he and I were inseparable. And so when I got tapped to go up there, he thought, 'Well, I'll go too.' Because nobody wanted to go up there to speak of. Nobody really wanted to go up there. This kid did everything for me. When I first joined the company he took me over to supply and said, 'You need this,' and 'You don't need that...' He showed me how to put magazines in bandoleers and to strip out plates from my flak jacket and to stuff my gas mask container with food instead of a gas mask. He also showed me how to take an NVA grenade and unscrew it and use the TNT to heat your chow with and C4 to heat food with.

On arriving at the ridge earlier that day, PFC Braden had initially reported to his 2nd Platoon Squad Leader, Lance Corporal Robert "Skip" Hedrick, a 20-year-old from Montana. Lance Corporal Hedrick, meanwhile, had been advised that he would have to reassign two of his men, one being required up on the Crow's Nest and another to help flesh out the seriously depleted ranks of 3rd Platoon on the southern slope. PFC Arthur had already put his hand up to go with his friend PFC Gentry up on the Crow's Nest, which left PFC Braden being sent to 3rd Platoon for the night. His "Buddy Plan" nemesis continued to haunt him and PFC Braden would once again be sent to serve with comparative strangers.

PFC Dale Braden: Arthur, he was acting fire team leader. I got up there and brought mail, and we all got our mail and I was sitting there with Arthur. He got some mail from home and he was really happy. Me and him was talking and Skip come over and he said, 'One of you guys have got to go up on the Crow's Nest and one of you guys go and stand lines with 3rd Platoon.' And Arthur says, 'I'll go up on the Crow's Nest,' and he was just happy as he could be.

LZ HAWK

The rambling sandbag bunkers of LZ Hawk were not only home to the battalion's artillery and 81-mm mortars, they also served as the battalion command post for Colonel Jack Davis. Additionally, it served as a "way stop" or staging point for Marines waiting for a lift on the next resupply helicopter heading out to the rifle companies operating in the hills and ridges.

One such transient was 2nd Lieutenant Bill Tehan, a 23-year-old Marine who had enlisted in 1962 in Baltimore, Maryland. Lieutenant Tehan had joined the Marines as an "enlisted" Marine at the age of 17. He had risen to the rank of Corporal in 2nd Force Reconnaissance before being selected for the Fleet Candidate Program in the Naval Reserve Officer Training Corps, a program

*Lance Corporal Robert 'Skip' Hedrick (left) and PFC Dale Braden.
(Credit: Robert Hedrick)*

to provide college education to especially promising Marines aspiring to be officers. He graduated from the University of Mississippi and was commissioned in June 1966.

On April 21, 1968, just five weeks ago, Lieutenant Tehan had been clearing out NVA bunkers on "Dead Man's Hill" near Khe Sanh. Armed with a .45 pistol, he had been covering an NVA bunker entrance while another Marine tossed a grenade into it. When the grenade went in, an NVA soldier immediately leaped out and Lieutenant Tehan shot him in the face at

Second Lieutenant William Tehan at LZ Hawk, May 1968.
(Credit: William Tehan)

point-blank range, killing him instantly. But the NVA soldier's muscles spasmed and squeezed the trigger in death, spraying a hail of bullets at Lieutenant Tehan. One of the bullets hit his canteen, another glanced off a smoke grenade attached to his shoulder strap, yet another hit the trigger guard of Lieutenant Tehan's pistol, jamming it onto his finger and rendering the weapon inoperable. A fourth bullet struck Lieutenant Tehan in the right temple, just to the right of his eye, severed the temporal artery and exited the back of his skull. Blood spurted out of the entry wound for a distance of 2 to 3 feet. Nearby Marines killed another eight NVA soldiers while a corpsman managed to pinch off the artery and slow the bleeding. Fortunately, a helicopter was currently inbound at just that moment and managed to hover while Lieutenant Tehan was lifted aboard. Within 15 minutes he was at a medical facility. He was unconscious for two days and, before his condition stabilized, received 26 pints of blood. He had three operations but amazingly was "up and around" on his feet within weeks. He was ordered to Bethesda Naval Hospital in Maryland. Apparently Colonel Davis was unaware of this, however, and contacted him via radio to see if he could take over as Commanding

Officer of Golf Company. The prospect of commanding his own company was too much for him to pass up, so Lieutenant Tehan ignored his medical orders. Thirty-five days after being shot in the head, he proceeded to LZ Hawk in anticipation of going out to join Golf Company.

2nd Lieutenant William Tehan: I had just gotten to LZ Hawk. I was there in the battalion CP at LZ Hawk waiting to go out to—I thought—Golf Company. I was back at LZ Hawk and so I was sort of an extra body at Hawk. I was an extra officer.

While there at LZ Hawk, Lieutenant Tehan quickly learned that one of the main reasons for the battalion's artillery battery being located there was to provide assistance to Khe Sanh in case of attack. Because of the terrain and the location of LZ Hawk, Foxtrot's own artillery (Bravo 1/12) was severely limited in its ability to deliver good support to the Marines defending the ridge.

2nd Lieutenant William Tehan: The reason that Bravo 1/12 was at LZ Hawk was to cover the batteries at Khe Sanh. In other words, if Khe Sanh took a ground attack, Bravo 1/12 covered the Khe Sanh batteries. Bravo didn't have a good lay of metal on Foxtrot Ridge for those guys. They could shoot, but they couldn't shoot very well because of the position of LZ Hawk to Foxtrot Ridge because it runs basically parallel to Route 9. Bravo could fire on the north side of the hill, but they couldn't give them any support to the east, up the hill; they couldn't fire over them and get to the valley to the west. They could only fire a little bit into the valley on the north side of the ridge. They were limited to where they could protect Foxtrot.

5 | THE EVENING OF MAY 27, 1968

As evening descended on May 27, 1968, the Marines readied their defenses. The Crow's Nest was now manned by its fresh complement of Marines. Among them were Corporal Howell, Lance Corporal Arthur, and PFCs Croft, Gentry, Nichols, and Blunk.

THE CROW'S NEST

PFC Croft was sorely disappointed after leaving his deep and solid foxhole facing Route 9 to arrive at the Crow's Nest and see the holes there.

> **PFC Robert "Hillbilly" Croft:** Well, when we got up there, I thought, 'Well this place is no good at all.' Of course they have the intelligence report, 'You're going to get hit,' or whatever. The holes were only like a foot-and-a-half deep, that old red dirt stuff. They had a little bit of dirt piled up in front of it. We scraped out a little bit more but just enough to crouch down in. Nothing to get down in. If we would have got up there a little earlier, me and my a-gunner, Mouse, we usually liked to really dig in, you know. But that dirt, it was just as hard as a rock.
>
> That was my first time on the Crow's Nest. I was on the opposite side of where the ridge was. When you went over the other side of the Crow's Nest, it came

back around. That was the ridgeline that came back around on the opposite of the road side of the ridge. There was ridge that come around over there. Well, we were facing that way. Because that's the way we figured they'd come because the company was behind us. And that was our hole there originally.

PFC Chris Gentry (left) and PFC Robert 'Hillbilly' Croft about to have a C-ration meal in the bush. (Credit: Robert Croft)

The Marines were taking their situation very seriously, perhaps nowhere more so than in the Crow's Nest. When they looked at their shallow holes and at the distance separating them from the rest of the company below, they knew they might soon be fighting for their very lives.

PFC Croft was well aware that, as a machine gunner, he would be an early and sought-after target if the enemy were to attack. He also knew that the machine gun ammunition, which came in long metal-linked belts, consisted of one tracer round every fifth bullet. These tracers glowed a bright red color as they left the barrel and allowed the gunner to see visually where the bullets were impacting. They were also useful in serving as a pointer, directing other Marines to a particular target. But most importantly he knew that the source of these tracers was immediately identifiable to the enemy, and they would then bring every weapon of theirs to bear on the Marine machine gun. PFC Croft used his own initiative to do something about that risk. He and PFC Espejo began removing the tracers and replacing them with conventional bullets.

PFC Robert "Hillbilly" Croft: I read that or somebody'd told me that. I said, 'Take all those tracers out, because this sounds like the real thing.' Actually the thing about those tracers, okay, they're good in the daytime if you're shooting to show everybody else where you're shooting but the tracer doesn't go as far as the regular round does. I always carried 200 rounds with me and a .45 and what grenades I could tote and everything else. And then my a-gunner, he carried 300 rounds and his M-16. Seems like we did carry a couple hundred more rounds up there but somebody brought some more ammunition up there at some time during that night.

Also at the Crow's Nest was 20-year-old PFC Mike Nichols, born and raised in Jonesboro, Arkansas. PFC Nichols had been in Vietnam since February and didn't like what he saw on the Crow's Nest either. He also knew that they were alone, probably too far away from the main perimeter to get back or receive support.

PFC Mike Nichols: It was a pretty good chunk of ter-rain because I remember when we were going up there that night, that afternoon you know, I said, 'Oh shit, we're a long way from the company if anything's going to happen.' I remember some of the older guys, been there longer, being worried about staying there that long. I was facing the company, laying right where you started down into the dip between the company and our position.

PFC Gentry left his position in the main perimeter facing the Crow's Nest to join those there. With him was his best friend PFC Arthur.

PFC Chris Gentry: So you walk down that depression and then you walk back up to the Crow's Nest, and if you call that the 6 o'clock I was at the 12 o'clock posi-tion on the other side, away from the company. Harold Blunk was in a foxhole to my right. And there was a machine gun over there too. Larry Arthur and I were in the same foxhole. Nichols was over to the left, somewhere around there.
I had a thousand rounds of M-16 ammunition. That's what I carried. I carried a thousand rounds the whole time I was over there. I just loved full automatic on that M-16. I probably had ten hand grenades and a white phosphorous grenade.

THE WESTERN FINGER

Down at the other end of the perimeter, at the western finger, the Marines of 1st Platoon were sending out their listening posts (LPs). An LP consisted of a small team of Marines, usually only three or four in number, whose job it was to position themselves along likely avenues of approach and sound the alert if they observed the enemy. This assignment was taken in turns by all the Marines of the company. On the night of May 27, two LPs were being sent out.

Private Don Schuck, an 18-year-old Marine from Indiana,

Air strikes hitting near Foxtrot Ridge.
(Credit: Louis Lopez)

who had arrived in Vietnam exactly one month ago, was one of the four Marines assigned to the LP whose destination was the grassy slope on the southwestern end of the western finger. Another was Lance Corporal Michael Cutri, one month shy of his 19th birthday, who had been in Vietnam now for a little over three months. Preparing themselves at dusk, they carried with them just their weapons, ammunition, grenades, and a radio. They had already removed the slings from their rifles, knowing that the metal clips where they attached to the weapon might rattle and give away their position. They stood quietly talking among themselves until darkness descended. Then they slipped quietly past the mortar pit of PFC Kinsella and Lance Corporal Walker until they reached a spot in the waist-high grass about 50 yards away and noiselessly crouched down in wait.

PFC Dave Kinsella: I remember them going out because they went right out in front of our hole. The LP was almost directly below us. They might have 50, 75 meters down there, down the hill. They weren't that far down.

At about the same time, Corporal Lockley led another three-man LP into its position on the northwestern slope of that same finger area. His destination was a spot somewhere on the other side of the bomb crater, which blocked their view and was in the general direction of the trail which the Marines had themselves used two days previously. One of the Marines was 19-year-old Lance Corporal Randy Huber from Reading, Pennsylvania.

Corporal Ron "Pappy" Lockley: So we decided to put an LP out there and I took two guys—I don't remember seems like it might have been Randy and some other guy—and we had a starlight scope. We just went right over past the bomb crater and a little ways down the hill so we wouldn't have a silhouette there. Where we were, it was just barren land and then down at the bottom of the hill it was real brushy and all. Where we were, it was just kind of barren. We just plopped down there and set in for the night and I had the second watch.

THE SOUTHERN SLOPE (away from Route 9)

Lance Corporal Mylin couldn't sleep and so quietly moved the short distance to the hole on his right where PFC La Bonte stood watch, sitting on the edge with his feet dangling into the hole. The two of them spoke quietly in whispers.

Lance Corporal Steve Mylin: I was in Tex's hole, he was just off to my right. We were bull-shitting. And they passed the word that we were going to get hit. It was a little after 11:00. They said we're going to get hit around midnight. We just kind of laughed because a lot of times they said that and we never got hit. They said, 'Everybody in their own holes, and everybody on full alert.'

THE COMMAND POST

Meanwhile, at the command post, the Marines of Foxtrot continued to be plagued with casualties. Corporal Dave Smith, the 81-mm mortar FO, had been diagnosed with likely malaria and was running a temperature of 103 degrees.

Gunnery Sergeant Ralph Larsen: Just about dark, Dave Smith came to me. He said, 'The corpsman wants to medevac me. I am dead sick.' And he was. He look like death warmed over. He had a bad fever and he was sick. And I said, 'Okay, give me your fire plan and so forth. I'll handle it.' I felt good enough about it; I'd just come back in the Marine Corps after being out on temporary disability. I left Hawaii and went to school out in California. One of them was Artillery, Air, and Naval Gunfire School. So, I was brushed up on that and I felt pretty comfortable with it.

6 | THE NIGHT OF MAY 27, 1968

The first few hours of darkness on the night of May 27 were quiet. A Marine remained awake and alert at every foxhole while nearby the other Marines assigned there slept on the ground.

THE CROW'S NEST

As midnight approached, PFC Nichols again picked up the starlight scope and turned it on. The eyepiece immediately began to glow that greenish hue of a 1960s vintage black and white television set. In another moment it had warmed up sufficiently to be operable and PFC Nichols raised the scope to his eye and scanned the terrain around the Crow's Nest as he had done every 15 to 20 minutes while standing watch. He made a startling discovery.

PFC Mike Nichols: We were standing watch along about where we were staying, facing the company. But it was a little bit more to our left, which would have been to the company's right. We had that old starlight scope up there and whoever was on watch, you know, would use it. They always told us to not keep it on all the time because it'd burn it up. The first movement that we had that night, it was like, oh, 11 o'clock, could have been earlier. On my watch, me—and it may have been me and Arthur or me and Gentry—anyway, on

our team's watch, I believe was the way it was. I took
that starlight scope and at one time there I counted
twelve. You could see them just a-walking, just like
lighted shadows, just walking like they were humping
stuff. Like ammo and stuff.

This was over to the company's right. As the company
was looking toward us, it would have been over to their
right, out in the bottom out there. It was a big valley.
That's what it was. I got to looking with that starlight
scope at the bomb craters and stuff down there, and
hell they were crawling like flies, you know. They were
all over the place down there. At that time they were
still packing ammo, getting into position in those
craters. They were packing their supplies into those
bomb craters. I didn't realize it to start with. I remember the first ones that I saw. Seems like there was only
six or seven. Then, hell, I got to looking around and
here was more. Like 12 at a time, you know, halfway
across the valley I would say. I'm going to guess probably about 500 meters. It was a real big valley; that
would have been probably 500 meters.

PFC Nichols made sure that everyone on the Crow's Nest
was awake and alert and, at the same time, radioed to the command post below that he had spotted enemy movement to
their south. The radio operator immediately responded, saying, "Wait one," while he got the "six," radio code for the
Commander Officer (CO), Lieutenant Jones. In a matter of seconds, Lieutenant Jones grabbed the handset and put it to his
ear.

PFC Mike Nichols: They woke the CO up and told
him. I remember the CO called up and I was talking to
him on my watch, him a-telling me what to do. Seems
like there was two or three of us—like me and Gentry
and Arthur—all on watch maybe at the same time.

For artillery forward observer, PFC Harold Blunk, the
sighting posed an interesting challenge. While PFC Blunk coor-
dinated the fire mission, PFC Nichols continued to observe
through the starlight scope, helping to direct the fire.

PFC Harold Blunk: One of the guys up on the Crow's Nest had a starlight scope and they spotted movement along the southeastern slope of the ridgeline. This was rather difficult area to bring in fire and I had never fired this close to the company. My best recollection is that this occurred about 2330 or so. We called in this fire mission and the guy looked through the starlight scope and was pointing out to me where they were at down there and I walked this artillery in and zeroed it in right on them. At that time there were NVA between us and the fire mission but we didn't know it. They hadn't started their attack but we were bombarding the shit out of them down there and I was calling in that fire mission. I concluded that fire mission. It was completely over. About 20 minutes later, all hell broke loose.

But I called in the fire mission. I had this feeling that— Oh, my God—they were moving along and we called in this fire mission. They thought, 'Hey, these guys have got us spotted and we might as well just hit them.' But no, that wasn't the case, they had already moved in closer to us.

Not only was PFC Blunk's fire mission successful in blunting this initial move of the enemy, it also allowed him to have a precisely preregistered spot to strike again at any time throughout the night with the sure knowledge of exactly where the rounds would land.

PFC Harold Blunk: To get that fire mission into the valley was very tricky because we were on a hill and I've got to walk that into the bottom there. That's why their attack was on a reverse slope where it would be very difficult to get artillery into. They're pretty clever that way. It was very difficult to get that fire on the southern slope but that fire mission was something that could be walked in and—at the end of it—you could just call up and say: 'Resume that fire mission on that target number.' That was already now registered. That was a big plus for us. To immediately come right back with that fire mission and then walk it around that side of the ridge.

The enemy at this stage were making no aggressive moves toward the ridge, and PFC Blunk's assumption—that the Marines once again caught an NVA unit trying to transit past them—seemed as reasonable as any. But a short time later, other sections of the Marines' defenses also began spotting movement.

THE WESTERN FINGER

Corporal Ron Lockley and his two fellow Marines were in their LP position on the northwest slope. Lockley had just been awakened for his turn on watch and sat silently for a few moments before deciding to scan the darkness with the starlight scope. He, too, was soon in for a surprise.

Corporal Ron "Pappy" Lockley: The next thing I did was I got the starlight scope out and started scoping out the area and… 'Great time of day!' I mean they were just hustling right down at the very bottom of that hill, on line, just encircling the hill down there. Couldn't hear any noise, though. You couldn't hear them. I was trying to count them and wake these guys and get information back at the same time. I got a count up in the 20s and so I know there was far in excess of 20 or 30.

Corporal Lockley and Lance Corporal Huber immediately advised Lieutenant Dito, who called for the 60-mm mortar tube in the center of the perimeter to begin firing down into the area of the NVA.

2nd Lieutenant Ray Dito: The first movement observed were the people trying to get to that cache of weapons because Huber had the starlight scope for my platoon. He was down at the end, where we bent around the end of the finger. He looked right down into that ravine, and he said, 'Lieutenant, we've got movement down here. We've got observed individuals moving around the base of the hill.' At that point, that's when I went to full alert status and I called Jones on the radio and told him that we've got movement down here and I put everybody on 100%. Then I told him we're going to need some illumination and I told him we're going to start using the mortars. As a small unit leader at that time I'd been taught to plan ahead, to make plans for your own defenses and to set these things up. So I had worked at various times, by this time in my tour over there, that when you occupy a night defensive position, you survey it, you figure out various scenarios that could happen and where the likely approaches were and how you're going to set up your defense.

Lieutenant Dito then moved down from his platoon command post to check the perimeter and stopped at the mortar team's position to prepare them to fire into the ravine, which led directly west from the finger of the ridge.

2nd Lieutenant Ray Dito: So I moved from my position down to the mortar tubes and I told the Chief, 'Chief, we got movement right down here. It's as tight as you can do it; you're going to have to hold it by hand.' I wanted them to fire about 90 degrees from where they were facing off to their right. I said, 'Chief, you're going to have to turn and fire over this way.' Then I got onto the LP [the one in front of Chief], and I asked them, 'Do you have any movement down there?' And they said, 'No.' So I said, 'Well, we've got movement around the side and you're going to have to come in but hold what you got right now.'

PFC Dave Kinsella: I think I had watch for something like 12 o'clock and 2 o'clock or something like that. My watch had just finished and I'd been just sitting on the edge of the mortar hole on the hill there. It almost seemed to me it was 12 o'clock and I'd woke up—I forget who the next guy was—for his watch and I'd just laid down and hadn't even got to sleep yet. That's when Lieutenant Dito came over with his radio man. He was calling down to the LP to see if they all secure. He told us when he first came over, you know, he put everybody on 100%. He said, 'We've got movement.' Somebody'd spotted the gooks on the finger. My recollection is he said they were coming up that finger to the west, the same trail that we had come up when we originally came up the ridge. Somebody had spotted them in the starlight scope and we were on 100%, everybody up. And he called down to the LP to see if they were all secure. Well, when he called them, he got the two clicks on the handset or whatever they were doing that everything was okay. He wasn't there long; he went off. We were all just, you know, everybody up with helmets and so on and we got in the hole.

Back on the other northwestern side, the mortars began raining down on the NVA soldiers spotted by Corporal Lockley using the starlight scope. But he soon discovered that the "blooming" effect on the scope, caused by the flash of the mortars impacting, rendered the scope ineffective for several long seconds and prevented him from seeing the mortars' effect.

Corporal Ron "Pappy" Lockley: Then we had a problem because at that point they wanted to fire some mortars down there so they started firing mortars. We were going to spot for them or try to, but every time there was an explosion, then you couldn't see anything with a starlight scope so you really couldn't get a good picture of what was going on. We knew that they were in the right area with their mortars. These were 60-mm, firing right out of our perimeter there. Fired several of those and I think maybe we might have shot some blooper [M-79 grenade launcher] rounds down in that area. At that point we decided it was time for us to pull back—and I've completely lost track of any kind of time frame. In fact, I couldn't tell you how long a time this was, but I want to say 15 minutes. It may have been 30; it may have been 10.

Back on the southwestern part of the finger, Lance Corporal Walker was fully aware of the sounds of mortars hitting at the base of the ridge directly behind him. These were being fired by the other mortar team, the one up near the CP. The area directly to Lance Corporal Walker's front remained quiet. He prepared to fire his mortar almost straight up and with a minimum amount of propellant so that the rounds would land at his designated target, only a few scant yards to the west.

Lance Corporal Alan "Chief" Walker: Then it got quiet again. Then somebody else came down to the line, and it may have been Ray Dito again or it might have been his platoon sergeant, and they said, 'Don't launch until we tell you to.' So I angled my mortar to damn near 90 degrees because I knew they were going to be very close. And I put a charge one. I could have put a charge zero but it may not have gone high enough to arm the fuse. So I angled it just very little and we waited.

The situation quickly changed when Lieutenant Dito, again in the area of Lance Corporal Walker's mortar team, heard an entirely different message from the LP to their front. When the Marines of the LP turned to look back at the ridge, they could see shadowy figures between themselves and the main perimeter of Foxtrot Company.

2nd Lieutenant Ray Dito: I was with my radio operator; Chafin was right behind me. He was just kind of hanging with me. I was sitting on the back of the hole and I had an M-16 with me. Then, the listening post says—I guess it was when the illumination rounds went up—he could see us clearly from his position. He said, 'There's movement between you and me.' And at that point I've figured out that this is pretty serious. I said, 'Well, I don't want you running through the movement at this point because there's liable to be some firing so you'll have to stay put.'

THE SOUTHERN SLOPE (away from Route 9)

Facing down the southern slope some 75 yards to the left of the LP, Sergeant Dave McCoy first heard the LP's radio call indicating they had seen NVA movement. It brought back a chilling reminder of similar attacks he had seen when serving with the 4th Marine Regiment on his previous tour of duty.

Sergeant Dave McCoy: Well, I was going to wake my radio man up at midnight. And I did wake him up. It was all quiet, no problems. Nothing was going on. And he got up. He was sleepy, you know. And I said, 'Are you awake?' He said, 'Yeah.' This was, like, a couple minutes after twelve. And I didn't hear him, you know, scurrying around or anything so I asked him again, 'Are you awake?' and he says, 'Yeah, I'm awake.' So I said, 'Okay, I'm going to get some sleep, but if you're too tired, wake me up.' So, I laid down and I hadn't even shut my eyes when the whispering started on the radio. That was that LP. And I can't remember right now his name—he was a buddy of mine. Sad, I can't remember his name. I can remember what he looked like. But he was down on that LP that night. And it was him on the radio. He was down on that LP and he called in on the radio and he said, 'There's movement all around us down here.' And then—you know it was real hard to make out on the radio—because you know I keyed in and I said, 'Come back. What were you saying?' I was whispering real low. And he said 'There's hundreds of them crawling on their stomach up the hill.' And I said, 'Holy shit!' At that time then the lieutenant from 1st Platoon got on the radio and he said, 'Repeat it,' and he came back on and said it and he said, 'What do you want us to do?' My thoughts were telling him, 'Get the hell out of there now.' But that lieutenant told him, 'I want you to stay there…' But I already knew what was going to develop. In fact, while I'm listening to the lieutenant, I'd already sent my radio man—he's the one that got all my guys up. The radio man went around there as soon as I heard that stuff going on. That's when I got everybody up in my platoon. Both sides, I got their asses up really quick because I knew what was coming.

THE EASTERN END (facing the Crow's Nest)

All around Foxtrot's perimeter defense, the Marines were preparing for the now likely enemy attack.

PFC Kevin Henry: I was asleep in the hootch and we got word, you know, 'Helmets and rifles, everybody in your holes. We got boocoo movement. First Platoon has boocoo movement.' And shortly thereafter, it might have been one o'clock in the morning but even though I wore a watch I wasn't concerned with what time it was. I was more concerned with, 'Okay, let's go.'

THE NORTHERN SLOPE (facing Route 9)

Weapons Platoon Commander Sergeant Pressler on the northern slope had a good vantage point from which to observe the area where Corporal Lockley's LP had first sighted the NVA. For the next several minutes, he sprinted back and forth from his position to the mortar team behind him, instructing them and directing their fire.

Sergeant Hubert "Dick" Pressler: They came from the point, down to my left. That's where they started coming through. That was the same trail we came up, same one. That's when I ran up there and directed the mortars to start firing back there. Then I ran back down to observe and then ran back up, calling them to where to shift their fire and then ran back down again and then up again. I was running back and forth.

THE COMMAND POST

At Foxtrot's command post, the situation was being coolly assessed by Lieutenant Jones.

1st Lieutenant James Jones: The initial manifestation of enemy presence was a mortar attack from the back side of 1st Platoon, in other words, the side closest to Route 9. We responded by firing 60-mm mortars because we had visual sighting of them. We could see them.

7 | FOXTROT AWAITS THE ATTACK

By this time, approximately 2:30 AM on May 28, every Marine of Foxtrot knew that their worries about remaining on the ridge had been well founded. Earlier, the NVA had been sighted (although the Marines couldn't be sure of what the NVA were doing) in the valley on the southern side. That movement had been effectively broken up by the artillery barrage directed by PFC Blunk. Next, there had been the movement sighted on the northern slope in the area of the trail leading up to the ridge. That, too, had been effectively countered by Foxtrot's own 60-mm mortars. Now, the LP on the southwestern area of the finger was reporting large-scale enemy movement—and even NVA soldiers between themselves and the company.

The Marines of Foxtrot Company were well-trained and experienced. They continued to hold their fire, knowing full well that their muzzle blasts were a dead giveaway to their position. Often the initial enemy probe was merely a feint, intended to draw their fire, thus allowing the NVA to locate their key defensive positions. These Marines would hold their fire until the last possible moment, defying every natural impulse coursing through their veins.

THE CROW'S NEST

PFC Croft, like the other Marines, had heard the earlier intelligence report about the likelihood of attack that night. He couldn't help looking around at the mere handful of Marines with him and wonder why there were so few. Before long, he began to hear noises out in the darkness but couldn't be sure his senses weren't playing tricks on him.

PFC Robert "Hillbilly" Croft: Well, we had some knowledge of it before. They were pretty sure. Because we were talking about it, 'Well, why don't they do something about it?' you know. Seems like it was about one or two o'clock in the morning that movement was started. We heard jabbering, you know how they do. We heard some jabbering and going on like they were kind of confused. So we thought, 'Well, we're hearing things,' there to start with.

Soon there was no doubt and the Marines knew the fighting was imminent.

PFC Harold Blunk: I was the only one who had a hootch up on the Crow's Nest. By hootch, I mean just a one-man poncho made into a little tent like we used to do. One of the other fellows that was up there, one of the things he did was to knock that down. He knocked down my hootch because of course it would have been silhouetted on the skyline. We were all up and alert and looking for them. There was nobody asleep at the wheel.

THE WESTERN FINGER

At approximately 2:45 AM, the dark silence out in front of Lance Corporal Alan Walker's mortar team was shattered by a series of brilliant flashes, thundering explosions and the sudden crackle of gunfire. Three NVA soldiers, carrying "satchel" charges full of TNT, leaped among the four-man LP crouched in the grass some 50 yards out from Foxtrot's perimeter. The Marines there quickly responded with rifles and grenades. In a shuddering quick series of explosions, the LP ceased to exist.

Lance Corporal Alan "Chief" Walker: And then we heard all that gunfire and explosions going off where the LP was. There was automatic gunfire and grenades. Then we knew they were really close. Then we could hear them. We could hear them crawling up the hill. It was pitch dark; it was really dark, which I'm glad it was—and we're all in our mortar pit. I was so afraid, I was glad it was dark. I put both of my hands under my armpits because I was shaking so hard. I didn't want the guys to know that I was afraid. If someone would have said, 'Run!' we would have gladly got the heck out of there that quick! I mean all of us would have. Then you could just hear them, and I ain't kidding you, that was the worst feeling of all. To hear the grass breaking and snapping, to hear them dragging themselves and their equipment up the hill, and you could hear them talking. That was so nerve-wracking. There were lots of them. We could just hear the labored breathing all up and down in front of us.

PFC Dave Kinsella: The elephant grass in front was about two foot tall, maybe. It was enough for, when they were coming up, you couldn't see them; you could hear them coming through the grass. When it was dark that night, you couldn't actually see them because they were crawling. You could hear the rustling of the grass and you could hear the noise. Everything was so chaotic that night. I was scared to death. I remember being in that hole on my knees and my whole body just trembling. I thought for sure we were all just going to die. I really did. I really thought it was over with that night. I really did.

Lance Corporal Alan "Chief" Walker: It was either Gil or Dave who said, 'Let's shoot!' But I said, 'There's nothing to shoot at; there's nothing out there.' I did have a claymore mine in front of us and I hit the plunger and nothing happened. And then either Dave or Gil said, 'Do it again,' and I did, but nothing happened. So then I just started pulling the wire back and here it was cut. Boy, I tell you, my heart really sank then. I was really afraid. I mean we all were. You could just hear them. You could hear their canteens, you could hear their cartridge belts, dragging stuff. I'm sure

they didn't know exactly where we were at. But then
one of them kept saying, 'Marine, surrender; Marine,
surrender.' Maybe that's not what he was saying, but
that's what it sounded like to me.

THE COMMAND POST

At the command post to the left of the action occurring at
the western finger, Gunnery Sergeant Larsen took up an
exposed position near Lieutenant Jones. He also double-checked
the fire plan for the 81-mm mortars that the malaria-stricken
Corporal Smith had handed to him earlier.

Gunnery Sergeant Ralph Larsen: We knew they were
heading toward us and so we were making preparations.
So I'm sitting there now, really paying attention to the
defensive fire plans. I'd gone around making sure the
people were awake and knew we were going to have
visitors. And then, I moved over closer to the CP. I didn't
have a hole there. Right behind me—I was facing out to
the south, maybe because that's where I first saw them
coming—right next to me was Lieutenant Heinz. All
night long he'd say, 'Get your head down, Gunny! Get
your head down!' Pretty soon he started irritating me
because he kept that up. Anyhow, I felt a little uncomfortable over there because I didn't have a hole. All I had
was my pack to lean my rifle on. All I was doing there
was I was ready to accept any orders that the Company
Commander gave because he had the radio. But before
they got there, Smith came back to me and he says,
'Okay, I'm going to try it. Go ahead and give it back to
me.' And he did. This guy—you know what it's like
being sick, if you had malaria—this was the kind of condition he was in, but he took it over. And so mainly what
I did was just pay attention to what I could pay attention
to and be ready to drive them off all alone or whatever it
took. To me, this was 'Custer's Last Stand.' I've been in
that position before and you're ready to do it. At the time
I said, 'Good, Let's get this over. Let's go.' You want it
and you don't, but you don't want to be sitting there,
waiting. Like the Chinese water torture.

8 | THE BATTLE BEGINS IN EARNEST

The Marines of Foxtrot Company were ready. They crouched or squatted in their foxholes, only their helmeted heads and shoulders visible; the smell of freshly dug earth was still strong. Their eyes and ears strained into the darkness.

THE CROW'S NEST

The 13 Marines up on the Crow's Nest waited nervously. The expected attack was clearly imminent.

PFC Robert "Hillbilly" Croft: The adrenaline was really going. We figured we were really going to get it. It sounded like everything was coming up there. Everybody was fairly quiet while they were getting ready. But we were about as ready as we could get. We wanted to make sure that everybody was awake and...here they come.

THE WESTERN FINGER

The agony of waiting was soon over for Lance Corporal Walker and PFC Kinsella. A red flare suddenly shot skyward from out of the darkness in front of them, and the battle began. The NVA soldiers leaped to their feet and began shooting. But the first wave had misjudged the distance they had crawled and believed the Marines were still further up the ridge's gentle slope. Their first burst of gunfire was over the Marines' heads. But the swarm of NVA soldiers ran as fast as they could through the hail of bullets the Marines fired in return.

Lance Corporal Alan "Chief" Walker: Then when the flare went up, they stood up and they must not have been more than four feet in front of us. What they did was shoot up the hill because they thought we were further up the hill. And hell, we just started shooting these guys right in the belly. We could have reached out and touched them. Once that flare went up and they started coming, they was running so hard that even on fully automatic we couldn't stop them. They were running between myself and Luebers, the rocket team to my right and also on the other side. As the flares were going off, and explosions, you could just see hordes of human beings running right over us. Within a few minutes, we were right in the middle of them. What we did, I had a pistol and I'm trying to reload magazines. We kept quiet, and then here's come another bunch at us and we'd start all in again. What I was afraid of was they'd come in behind us. And I kept looking back. Then the battle really did start. Everybody was into it, at least on the LZ.

PFC Kinsella shouldered his rifle easily and comfortably, having grown up around guns and having hunted since he was a boy.

PFC Dave Kinsella: They were fairly close. When I did catch a few of them in the illumination—you know the popup flares and they would light everything up for a short period of times—that's when I caught a couple of them. I shot one guy coming and running up in front of the rocket team next to us to our right. I saw him and shot him. That was an officer somebody said; he had two stars on the brass buckle. They got real close. I'd say they got within 20 yards. They were throwing those satchel charges, that TNT, whatever it was.

Basically, I had about eight grenades and I think I threw every one of them. I threw all my grenades and then I had an M-16 and I think I had two bandoleers: 16 magazines of ammo and I went through about 8 of those. I was just steadily spraying, full automatic. Just jamming one in after another, just spraying, time to time there, when I'd get the movement down in front of us. I think Gil Leonard was doing the same thing and Chief, he only had a .45. I can't put a time frame on it because everything was happening so quick. I really don't even remember how long we were in that hole. Chief said we were in the hole for about an hour or so after this had all started.

Lance Corporal Alan "Chief" Walker: Prior to this, when they were crawling up in the grass, that had to be the worst. But once the shooting started, then your training and your everything just kicks in. It's automatic. But, boy, the waiting part was the worst. It wasn't the soldiers, once they started running through us, but boy it was that waiting. To me it was the absolute worst of it.

Once the shooting started, I ain't kidding you, they literally ran through, right through the two positions. I know Dave and Gil they were just pouring lead into the poor bastards and it didn't even stop them, didn't phase them. Of course they were falling down dead but there was just so many of them.

PFC Dave Kinsella: Everything was so chaotic. We didn't know what was going on anyplace else other than right where we were. I really didn't know what was going on up in the Crow's Nest or on the north side.

Lance Corporal Alan "Chief" Walker: Then it kind of slowed down again. By then we had quite a few 'gooks' laying right in front of us, all around us, dead of course. And then we started grabbing their ChiComs and throwing them back at them. We also used a couple of their AKs until we ran out of magazines. I don't know how long this might have been. Might have been a half hour or may have been 45 minutes, maybe even less.

THE SOUTHERN SLOPE (away from Route 9)

PFC Braden, newly assigned to stand lines with 3rd Platoon, found himself in a foxhole a short distance to the left of Lance Corporal Walker and PFC Kinsella. His position too was under heavy assault.

> **PFC Dale Braden:** When it first happened, I was down with 3rd Platoon, down on the lower part, right where they come up. We joined onto 1st Platoon. I was facing the other way from Route 9. There was maybe two more holes between where I was at and where 1st Platoon joined 3rd around on that side. I was standing lines with 3rd Platoon that night.
>
> I knocked one guy down at least three times. He had a satchel charge and he was trying to get to our hole. He was about 30 yards away. He just come up screaming. When they popped that popup [flare] they was crawling on their bellies, but when they popped that flare they jumped up and started running. I guess they figured we'd already seen them...and they'd get there quicker running that crawling. I know the first shot had to take him out, but I had to hit him three times. I knew for sure I hit him three times. The rest of them, you know you'd hit people and they'd fall and there'd be somebody right behind him. That's just the way it was on our end of the hill.

THE COMMAND POST

The Marines' observation about the action slowing down after a while was very accurate, although most of them had no idea why the NVA had inexplicably slowed their attack. The answer lay with Gunnery Sergeant Larsen, the veteran of the Korean War. The night of the battle, he found himself in the rather odd position of being something of a spectator. Because he was in the CP group, he couldn't fire for fear of hitting a fellow Marine. So he was left to wait, to watch and to listen while the battle raged all around him. But a man of action like Gunnery Sergeant Larsen found that very difficult.

Gunnery Sergeant Ralph Larsen: Really what happened is I carried a pencil flare launcher in my pocket and I had two or three colors, little bitty things, probably about like your little finger. This is the stuff that comes in a pilot's emergency kit. It's got a little spring thing you pull back and release and hits the little cap and, 'boom,' off it goes. I picked it up down at Quantico one time. I was a skydiver and the parachute loft there had some 'excess' so I had myself one. And I carried it for quite a while. So when I went to Vietnam, it was one of the things I took along with me. At one time things were kind of nasty and I just got to wondering myself if I shot one of those little green flares if it would make a difference. So I moved over and shot it, and it did seem to quiet things down for a bit.

I'm laying there. I don't have a hole anyhow and I don't have anything to do. I'm feeling like I ought to be up there probably firing a rifle or shooting a machine gun or something. I thought, 'What can I do?' And there was really nothing you can do, except to be ready for 'Custer's Last Stand,' as I like to think of it. Anyhow, I thought I'd just try it because in Korea, Chinese always, for some reason or other, always use green when they were going to cut off an attack. It just seemed always to be the signal. You'd see that green, you'd say, 'Oh boy! We're getting a break now.' So that's the reason I fired that green one. And that's all I fired. Then later on, I tried it again and it didn't do anything. I did do it later on and it did nothing. And that was it. End of story. Nothing to it. Very simple.

When Gunny Larsen fired the green pencil flare into the sky, pandemonium and confusion soon broke out in the ranks of the North Vietnamese soldiers attacking the Marine positions. Many of the NVA ceased firing, and scores of them actually turned around and started back down the hill while screaming North Vietnamese officers and noncommissioned officers attempted to restore order and resume the attack.

Lieutenant James Jones: We didn't want to show our position so we fired mortars and, simultaneously with that, the LP was hit on the other side of the hill. The first assault wave was launched by aid of three [red] flares as I recall across the length of the perimeter to include the Crow's Nest. And it was while we were trying to respond to that, we fired the [green] flare, which broke their attack. We had inadvertently stumbled on their withdrawal 'comm' [communications] signal. And that gave us some precious time to get ourselves reorganized.

The Marines all knew they were hopelessly outnumbered and outgunned by the attacking force of NVA. They desperately needed supporting arms—artillery and mortars—to tilt the balance in their favor. A few moments earlier, Corporal Smith, despite his malaria, had taken his maps and his fire plan back from Gunnery Sergeant Larsen. The role of forward observer for the 81-mm mortars back at LZ Hawk was again in his safe—though occasionally shaking from fever—hands.

Corporal Dave Smith: The next thing that happened was Lieutenant Jones started saying, 'We need 81s down there.' So I started calling back to the [mortar] platoon. When I first called them—at this point it's probably two, three in the morning—it's late. The funny thing is that, when I called back to the platoon, the radio operator back there said, 'Is the stuff really necessary?' And I said, 'Yes, It's necessary. Get everybody up, would you?'
The guns [mortars] back there, with our platoon, they did a great job all night. I mean we were on top of the hill, but these guys were back there and they didn't miss a shot.

EASTERN END, Facing the Crow's Nest

Sergeant Quinn was still settling into his new job as Platoon Commander for 2nd Platoon. Once the firing started, the crescendo of noise continued to increase. It was clear that Sergeant Quinn's good friends back on the western finger were catching the brunt of the attack.

Sergeant Joseph Quinn: I remember the flare that night. We were all set up that night. I remember the flare going off and thinking, 'What the hell is that?' I'm not sure where I was at the time because I was moving around a bit then. I was going around, trying to get names and stuff because I didn't know the platoon. I was trying to find out who was who, where all the personnel were.

The flare went off and then the shit hit the fan. It was somewhere over between the LP and 1st Platoon. Somewhere over there, I thought. Maybe it was in the tree line, I can't be sure. Then we started hearing the popping. They were the rounds. Then it really hit the fan.

Lance Corporal Richard Cutbirth, home on leave, just prior to shipping out to Vietnam, December 1967. (Credit: Mrs. R. Cutbirth)

In the machine gun position, both Marines waited expectantly. Lance Corporal Richard "Dickie" Cutbirth had been in Vietnam since early December and had seen plenty of action in that time. But this was clearly developing into something far bigger than even he had seen. A 19-year-old from Missouri, he was characteristically unruffled by it all, though. He made sure the M-60 was ready to go, checked that the ammunition was nearby and clean, then shrugged his shoulders and smiled an "Okay, Let's get it on," look at the Marine manning the trigger, PFC Kevin Henry.

PFC Kevin Henry: First Platoon was clearly catching it. All the tracers and everything that was going up in the air was coming off to my right, which was where 1st Platoon was. I clearly knew that the shit was going to hit the fan, and all I was doing was watching in front of my position.

9 | THE BATTLE CONTINUES IN THE EARLY HOURS

It had taken only a few moments for the NVA to regroup and commence their attack in earnest. Now they came surging forward in unbelievable numbers. From nearby ridges and hilltops, NVA soldiers lobbed rocket propelled grenades (RPGs) at the Marines. Designed to knock out tanks, the RPGs' explosive charge was bigger than a football and its concussive force was enormous. It is estimated that the NVA fired 400 of these RPGs into the tiny perimeter of Foxtrot Ridge. They also threw hundreds of Chinese Communist-supplied hand grenades, which the Marines referred to as "ChiComs." The explosive head was mounted on a wooden handle, which contained a string-like pull cord and a screw-off cap on the end. The NVA would thus unscrew the cap and pull the cord, which detonated a striker and lit the fuse. Unlike the Marines' M-26 hand grenade, the ChiCom's fuse burned visibly like a firecracker fuse. In addition, the NVA were heavily armed with automatic weapons. Most of the assault troops carried AK-47 assault rifles (or their Chinese-manufactured equivalent), while hundreds of RPD light machine guns and scores of heavy-caliber machine guns added their firepower.

THE CROW'S NEST

The Crow's Nest provided a box seat view of the action unfolding on the ridge below, although it was probably the world's most dangerous box seat.

PFC Harold Blunk: And then the shit hit the fan. I mean it hit the fan simultaneously everywhere. I looked down at Foxtrot Ridge, and it was like fireworks going off overhead. I can't describe it any other way. There were just explosions all over, inside, the perimeter. It was just lit up down there from RPG rounds and other ordnance exploding. We thought we were on our own. We were in the Alamo. We were fighting 'Custer's Last Stand' because the company was being wiped out. That was what it looked like. It looked impossible for those guys to survive down there.

Corporal Kevin "Canadian" Howell: It opened on the other side. It didn't open on the Crow's Nest side. We saw movement, but not the in-force movement that the other side got. We heard, you know, like an FPF [final protective fire: a last ditch defensive measure wherein each Marine fires into pre-designated zones] is going on. We said, 'Oh God, the shit has started.' But where are they? Because what we're looking at is light probes. And what the company on the other side was looking at was a mass attack. Of course, when you're in a position where everything's happening behind you, and you hear all this noise, it was just like: silence . . . *pop, pop . . . kawhoom!* To me, the sound behind me is the company getting slaughtered. In my mind the entire company was the Alamo, and we were kind of like an outpost. I couldn't understand why we didn't have more people on the LP/OP since that was going to be the critical terrain feature. You always want to take the high ground, so they should have gotten at us first.

PFC Chris Gentry: None of our claymores worked. Not a single claymore fired. I had one up there with the handset in my foxhole, and I tried to set it off. I can't tell you now whether the electric line had been severed or whether it just failed to fire.

PFC Harold Blunk: Meanwhile, we're getting hit up there. It's just gunfire, ChiCom grenades. Where Arthur was, there were satchel charges. It was like terror in the night. At one point we were being shot at so intensely that my map got shot up. Two or three of us just hunkered down in this hole and the dirt was coming in the hole from the rounds hitting the edge of the hole. Heavy machine gun fire coming in. I wanted to stand up and shoot back, but this was just intense machine gun fire. The one fellow who was in the center of the hole just stuck his M-16 up out of the hole and fired frantically a clip of ammunition down the hill. There were NVA in front of us, and my biggest fear was not having a full magazine in my weapon. You think, 'My God, what if there's only three or four rounds left.? There's not going to be enough rounds to stop the onslaught.'

PFC Robert "Hillbilly" Croft: Then the first thing we saw was that little flash. You know when they pulled a cord on a ChiCom, there was a flash when that striker was pulled. And then they started lobbing them in on us. You know, if they would've overrun us, they would've been on top of the company. So, we couldn't pull back.

The Marines on the Crow's Nest suffered their first casualty when a grenade landed next to 18-year-old PFC Lawrence Arthur in a foxhole.

PFC Chris Gentry: Larry fought like a demon and was hit within the first hour of the battle. We had a very little foxhole. We were sitting as close as two people could sit together. I was in the foxhole with him when he was hit. It was just one of those firefight deals. There was an explosion. We were being shot at by a machine gun and he was hit. I can't tell you if he was shot first or killed by a grenade. It might not even have been a grenade; it might have been a satchel charge. Larry was hit within the first hour of the battle.

PFC Mike Nichols: But anyway, I remember that one: they chucked it and it hit right in the hole with Arthur ...and went off. I remember I rolled him over, I scooted back, crawled back and rolled him over. It had blown right through his midsection.

The Marines of Foxtrot 2/3 wait for a helicopter lift and another operation. LZ Hawk, April 1968. (Credit: Author's Collection)

There was no corpsman on the Crow's Nest. The 12 remaining Marines were in a fight to the death, locked in battle with hundreds of NVA troops assaulting them from every direction. There was no time for ceremonies, no time for farewells. The Marines there simply carried on with the fight.

THE WESTERN FINGER

Because of the gentler slopes and the nature of the terrain, the western finger was being particularly hard hit. The Marines at the southwestern corner were now out of ammunition and using rifles and grenades stripped from the dead NVA soldiers lying nearby.

PFC Dave Kinsella: It was so chaotic at that point.

There was so much noise, people were yelling. The gooks were yelling and hollering. At that point they were already behind us, which we didn't even realize, already on the LZ. They were up in that area. They overran the finger from what I understand. They got through at the very end of the ridge.

A grenade came hurtling into the mortar pit, and the four Marines all managed to leap to safety before it exploded. PFC Kinsella, assuming the others were right behind him, moved backwards, seeking a protected position on the other side of the ridge's crest.

PFC Dave Kinsella: After that I really don't know how long we were in the hole, but I do remember seeing the grenade. You know, you could see those ChiCom grenades, the spark trailing off of them. And that thing came right between me and Gil Leonard. I went out the west of the hole. I jumped up out the west side just as the grenade went off. And Gil went out the front of the hole; I remember seeing him go out the front. That's when I took off. I went across the LZ to the north side and got, basically, on the other side of the LZ. I thought everybody else had left.

2nd Lieutenant Ray Dito: Just about that time in the light of one of the illumination rounds, three NVA came into the glow of the illumination from behind us. They were saying, 'We're friendlies. We're friendlies.' They pretty much jumped in the hole with the two of us, and we took care of these NVA. Now, they didn't have rifles; they were covered with TNT. They were sappers. They weren't sure exactly where our lines were until the illumination round went up. They were walking, they were not crawling, at that point. They were a little disoriented as to our exact position. Whatever their job was, I guess they were looking for obstacles or some-thing, but there weren't any. We had nothing. At that point, I realized, 'This is not good.' So, I told Chafin, 'Let's pull back. We'll go to the other side of the perime-ter. We'll move past the LZ and we'll just go over the side of the lip of the hill to get into a defilade position.

Lieutenant Dito pulled back over the crest of the ridge to the northern slope, but he overestimated the distance to the other side. In the confusion of all the shooting and the explosions, he tumbled down the slope, ripping the handset from the radio and disabling it.

2nd Lieutenant Ray Dito: Well, we went too far. Straight across from that side of the ridge there was a steep drop-off. Well, Chafin and I fell off the top of the ridge. We tumbled down the hill, probably 25 to 35 yards, together. I had been holding onto the radio handset, and I jerked it right out of the radio. I didn't talk over the phone to Jones again that night. So Chafin and I now, we're at the bottom of the hill, well outside the lines and I said, 'This is even worse than being on the exposed side of the lines. They're going to open up on us.' So I told him, 'All right, let's start crawling back up and we'll announce ourselves,' because we didn't feel that there was anybody between us and the perimeter at that point. So we crawled back up. I think Tex was on that side of the hill, so I yelled out to him, 'Hey, it's Lieutenant Dito and we're coming back in.' They weren't firing, there was nothing going on on that side.

In fact, when we got back inside the lines, we kind of set up in a little position behind the lines there in the elephant grass on the east side of the LZ. Chafin and I we set up right there, because he was passing out grenades. Then, when I came back in the lines with Chafin, I told him, 'Go up to the CP and get as many grenades as you can.' It was just crazy because he disappeared, and I'm sitting there by myself now with no communications, behind that side of the perimeter.

Meanwhile, Corporal Lockley's LP had pulled back to their regular position, back and to the left of the bomb crater. He could hear the pitched battle taking place on the southwestern slope behind him and became increasingly uncomfortable with the relative quiet in his own sector. He knew that the mortar fire had stopped the first group of NVA, but what if there were others?

Corporal Ron "Pappy" Lockley: I don't know. You just don't have any concept of time during all this kind of goings-on. Anyway, we pulled back up to the top at that point. I was just still real uncomfortable because we got up to the top, and we started to get small arms fire. We could hear it on the other side of the hill. There was so much going on, and I was just so uncomfortable with that bomb crater. At that time, we weren't taking any fire at all on our corner. I just had a vision of them, by the hundreds, just creeping up the side of that hill.

So I grabbed a couple of guys and the starlight scope and I said, 'Let's go and just take a peek at what's over there on the other side of that crater.' I didn't take my rifle because I had that big old starlight scope; that's why I took those two guys. I said, 'Y'all protect me.' So we dropped just inside that crater, so we wouldn't be silhouetted and worked our way around to our right around the edge, just inside that bomb crater. When were got right to the other side, one of them threw a grenade in on us. So we high-tailed it back around. The strangest thing was when we got back and was coming out of the bomb crater—I was the last one of the three out—I heard somebody behind me. We heard the grenade go off and some small arms fire and I heard, I would have swore, somebody behind me say, 'I'm hit.' And I twirled around and I was just face-to-face with a NVA soldier there and he had his rifle locked in his hip …and all I had was a starlight scope. He unloaded, but he missed me.

Another Marine dispatched the NVA soldier, who some-how had missed Corporal Lockley, even though at point-blank range. Corporal Lockley then went back to his previous location but found that his hole had been taken. The only scant protection available was the trash pit, only a couple of feet deep and half-filled with empty C ration cans.

Corporal Ron "Pappy" Lockley: At that point I was standing right in front of our machine gunners' position. But anyway we got on out of there, and I got back up to where I had been and there was really no place for me. We had a trash pit there and it was about half-full or three-quarters-full. It was right next to a foxhole and I had two new guys in that foxhole in my squad. They were in a hole, and the only hole I could find next to them was the trash pit. I laid prone in the pit and since these guys were both fairly new, I was keeping an eye on them.

Directly to his right was the machine gun, set up just behind the bomb crater and manned by Lance Corporal Bacote. Also, somewhere over there was Lance Corporal Huber.

Corporal Ron "Pappy" Lockley: Sometime after I got to the trash pit, I recall small arms fire coming from somewhere to my right. I want to say from about our machine gun position. The first position was around the corner from where we were and just behind the crater, and the next position was down close to the brushy tree line area. This small arms fire was chewing up the ground around the trash pit I was in, and I could literally feel the rounds as they whizzed past my head. I heard Moses yell that he was hit and right after that crying out for someone to help him. This was in the machine gun position. I was unable to see anyone in that area and assumed the area was still secure since there was no word from anyone. In hindsight I think our perimeter may have been breached on that side as well. This would have been the area where Moses and Randy Huber were and some others I can't recall.

Lance Corporals Moses Bacote and Randy Huber were both dead. Their sector of Foxtrot's defense was now silent.

The Marines were inflicting a heavy toll on their attackers, but they were being overwhelmed by the sheer number of NVA troops committed to the battle. With the adrenaline coursing through their bodies and in their heightened state of alert, many of the Marines of Foxtrot experienced the events as if in slow motion.

Lance Corporal Jim Chafin: There was a big bomb crater there, huge crater. And the gooks would go into that crater and then come up on the ridge. For a while it was like a popup shooting gallery, with them coming up. I remember one gook, he had a ChiCom in his hand. It seemed like, no matter how many times I hit him, I knew I was hitting him because I could see his helmet spin. I could see his shoulders flinch, but he kept coming. He just kept coming; he wouldn't go down. I fired and I fired and I fired. I don't know if he was on opium or what, but he just kept coming. He wouldn't drop. Finally he did drop.

The area occupied by Corporal Steve Baker and Lance Corporals Bill "the Bear" Grist and Michael "Smitty" Smith was also under attack and directly in the path of the advancing NVA soldiers. RPG rounds smashed into the ground around them and a hail of machine gun fire tore the dirt up around their foxhole. Corporal Baker and Lance Corporal Smith continued to rise up out of their foxhole, regardless of the risk, and fire long bursts of fully-automatic M-16 rifle fire into the charging figures to their front. Lance Corporal Grist did the same but used his M-79 grenade launcher at point-blank range with deadly effect. Within moments, however, Lance Corporal Grist was shot in the head; his death instantaneous. Lance Corporal Smith's death took longer; receiving a gunshot wound to the stomach.

Lance Corporal Jim Chafin: The corpsman, he went out and he tried to help Smitty. Smitty was done. He knew it, but he didn't want to let go. He was holding on for his last breath. He knew enough to…, he had a picture of his wife and his baby. He died with the picture in his left hand and holding his guts in with his right.

Corporal Baker had been shot too, badly wounded but still alive. Drifting in and out of consciousness, he confirmed that his two friends were indeed dead and then began crawling backwards, back toward the center of the ridge.

PFC Kinsella made it back over the crest of the ridge from his mortar position into the tall grass of the center. He found there a number of other Marines. He also heard the pained cry of a wounded Marine further down the ridge.

PFC Dave Kinsella: The gooks were already actually behind us somewhat and in front of us. The LZ was almost directly behind us. I ran across the LZ back over to the other side where the elephant grass was tall over there. There was a number of guys huddled up over there. I don't know how long we were there. It was just a short period of time, and we just sort of huddled up. That's when I heard the other guy who was on the LP out on the LZ. He was kind of on the fringe there where the LZ had been cleared, where the elephant grass was tall and he was laying out there. He was calling for help. We couldn't really see him. We could hear him. Some illumination went off, and we could see him out there then, and could see that he was one of us. He might have been, maybe 20 or 30 yards out. And that's when I tried to get some of those guys to go help me. You know, 'We got to go get him!' Nobody would move.

PFC Kinsella darted out to the wounded Marine alone, quickly grabbing him and pulling him back to safety. But in the few seconds that he was gone, the other Marines had vanished. He was again forced to assist the wounded Marine unaided.

PFC Dave Kinsella: Finally I just took off and I went out there and grabbed him. He had been shot through the leg, I remember that. He had been shot through the left thigh, upper left thigh. I remember grabbing him by the wrist and just pulling as hard and as fast as I could. The gooks were up there, but I didn't realize it at the time. They were somewhere around on the LZ. I guess I was just lucky that maybe they didn't know who I was or they thought I was one of them, or I don't know what was going on. And there may not have been any of them. I don't think I was in the illumination during it either. I think it was dark. But I just remember getting back over to where I'd been, where the guys were huddled, and everybody was gone. There was nobody there to help me.

Lieutenant Dito had received his resupply of grenades and tossed them at the NVA soldiers who had penetrated into Foxtrot's position. Once out of grenades—and realizing he had been out of contact with Lieutenant Jones since he had pulled the handset from the radio earlier on—Lieutenant Dito made his way back to the command post.

2nd Lieutenant Ray Dito: And then Chafin comes back and he's got half a dozen grenades. So we sit there, and I say, 'All right.' We could hear the North Vietnamese talking now; we were within earshot, and they weren't talking loudly. I started taking the pins out. I started throwing grenades into the LZ from where I was. I wasn't throwing them down the hill.

I hadn't talked to Jones, and I hadn't moved since the time we'd gotten back in the lines. I assumed the NVA came through where the mortar position was. I figured they had just followed up their initial penetration with a larger group and had set up and were making a move from the area of the LZ, which was right behind the mortar position.

After I had thrown a few, then a ChiCom landed about three feet from Chafin and myself. They threw one over at us. We just flattened ourselves out. It went off, and I took some shrapnel in the back and Chafin took a little in his hand, but neither one of us was seriously hurt by it. They weren't taking a chance; they didn't know where we were. All they knew was that somebody was throwing grenades at them from somewhere over on that side of the perimeter.

Once we got through with those grenades, I figured, 'Well, I'd better try to get up to the CP.' So, I told Tex, 'They penetrated up to the LZ, so look over your left shoulder and protect that side of the perimeter because they're in between us and the end of the finger where first squad and the gun was.'

With Lieutenant Dito and the others now gone, PFC Kinsella dragged the wounded Marine over to the northern side of the perimeter and stopped for a moment to catch his breath.

PFC Dave Kinsella: They had all evidently pulled back farther because there was a path. I remember there was a path along the holes on that north side of the ridge. I got him over there, and we laid down there for a

PFC "Tex" La Bonte (right) and other Marines of Foxtrot 2/3 on a truck convoy in April 1968. (Credit: Author's Collection)

minute. Then they threw a grenade in right next to us in the elephant grass. I was laying next to him and, when they threw the grenade in, I saw it come in real close. It was within, like ten feet. I rolled over on top of him, trying to get away from it, and I believe that he got hit again in the wrist. He had a wound in his wrist then from the shrapnel, in his left wrist. It was at that point that I was trying to get him up the hill. Guys were running up that path, coming from the finger pulling back up the hill, and I was trying to stop them and get them to help me; nobody would even stop. I was real frustrated. I remember trying to get him up on my shoulder. He was a big guy; he had to weigh 200 pounds. He was a big guy, and it was hurting him too much. I ended up dragging him up the path, up the hill to a corpsman, up towards the CP group just below where the saddle was.

THE NORTHERN SLOPE (facing Route 9)

Sergeant Dave McCoy was near the middle of the perimeter, just behind the command post and facing south, when a round—probably an RPG or a mortar—exploded near his feet. It literally blew him into the air and backwards. He landed on the northern slope and tumbled down its steep incline.

Sergeant Dave McCoy: After they blew the hole down there, they blew the LP and they started moving up toward 1st Platoon. There were quite a few of them moving up toward 1st Platoon. Right away they were almost to the 1st Platoon lines. I mean a group of them, enough where you could see them in the dark among all those gunshots and explosions and all that stuff, but you could see them moving. They were almost to 1st Platoon, when that blast caught me. It blew me straight back, way up in the air. I sailed out of our positions and down that hill and back toward where La Bonte was.

I think I could honestly see our holes as I was flying through the air. I know I probably didn't; but I imagined seeing them because I was flying through the air for a long time. When I came down, it wasn't where I wanted to come down at.

Sergeant McCoy had his helmet torn from his head and was bleeding profusely from his facial wounds. He eventually slid to a stop some 30 yards down the northern slope of Foxtrot Ridge. His cartridge belt and ammo were gone, but he still clutched his rifle. As he looked around him, illuminated in the flashes of the explosions and the gunfire, he realized he had landed in the midst of a group of NVA soldiers moving forward in their attack.

Sergeant Dave McCoy: When I went in the air, I remember I had my rifle in the air and it didn't take any damage. I've got no idea where my helmet went, but it saved my head because I can remember a really big blow to my helmet. I got a few pieces in the face, and I got one chunk in the side of my face. I hit the hill once or twice and then I rolled over backwards and I rolled down a couple more somersaults down the hill and came to a stop down there. I guess I was almost face first. I can remember all that and I can remember flying through the air. When I came down, I didn't have any time to feel any pain because they started shooting at me right away.

There were eight North Vietnamese standing there. They started shooting. All I had left was my rifle. When I started sliding down the rest of the way, there was all these guys in front of me, and I thought for sure I was dead meat. I really did. There was no way I thought I'd ever get back up to our positions. I emptied my magazine out on those eight guys and hauled ass up that hill, screaming the whole way for La Bonte because I knew I was somewhere near his hole.

Miraculously, somehow Sergeant McCoy managed to scramble back up the ridge and through the Marines' lines. He was shot twice in the legs but kept going.

Sergeant Dave McCoy: Coming back to La Bonte's hole was where I caught the two of those in the lower calf of my leg. I didn't get hit again for quite a while. We were tossing grenades on them. They were coming up the south side. My biggest concern that whole night was that guys were staying down in their holes. Because they were pounding us. They were really pounding us. Anybody that knew me there probably saw me at one time or another, telling them to 'Get your heads up. They're still coming.'

THE SOUTHERN SLOPE (away from Route 9)

Meanwhile, the southern slope was also under heavy attack. Lance Corporal Kinkaid fed ammunition into the M-60 machine gun and the NVA quickly homed in on them with their RPGs.

Lance Corporal Robert Kincaid: Charlie Kohler opened up fire with the machine gun, and I fed the ammo for him. We started getting some RPG hits around our hole and we started attracting, like a magnet, their fire. And there was a sergeant from weapons platoon—maybe a corporal—and he slithered over into our foxhole with us and he had an M-16. The RPGs grew real thick there. I remember some pencil flares going overhead, some gook pencil flares. I heard a bugle. I remember a bugle.

Nearby, Lance Corporal Mylin could hear a machine gun firing long, long bursts from somewhere down on the finger.

Lance Corporal Steve Mylin: What I remember from when it started was that—I thought it was somebody from 1st Platoon—somebody kept shooting. I guess it was a machine gun. I mean, they never let up. They just kept shooting, firing continuously. I kept thinking, 'Man, that's just going to draw the gooks and they're going to wipe that out in no time'. That thing just kept firing and firing and firing and firing. Then those rockets started coming in, and all hell just broke loose. We weren't doing much in our fighting hole except trying to dodge the bullets.

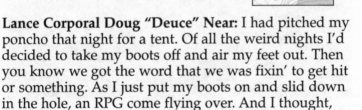

EASTERN END (facing the Crow's Nest)

Lance Corporal Doug "Deuce" Near: I had pitched my poncho that night for a tent. Of all the weird nights I'd decided to take my boots off and air my feet out. Then you know we got the word that we was fixin' to get hit or something. As I just put my boots on and slid down in the hole, an RPG come flying over. And I thought, 'Damn, what a time to take my boots off!'

Meanwhile, despite all that incoming barrage of enemy fire, several Marines crawled from hole to hole, checking those in their unit. Usually it was just a quick, whispered, 'You guys okay here?' Lance Corporal Hedrick was one such squad leader moving throughout his sector of the perimeter. There was a particular need for more grenades back down on the western finger, so Lance Corporal Hedrick went round gathering up what could be spared and then delivered the dozen or so now-priceless items.

Lance Corporal Doug "Deuce" Near, Phu Bai, South Vietnam, 1968.
(Credit: Robert Hedrick)

THE COMMAND POST

By this time Lieutenant Dito—out of radio communication since the opening minutes of the battle—had made his way up from the western finger to advise Lieutenant Jones of the crisis down there.

2nd Lieutenant Ray Dito: So then Chafin and I crawled up to where Jones was. I don't know how much time had passed by this point; that's kind of a blur. I'll guess this is about an hour later. I told Jones, 'This is the situation. We've been penetrated down near the LZ. I've got some men cut off on the end but I'm going to go down and try to turn it around and enclose that side of the LZ.' So then Chafin stayed there and I crawled back down.

1st Lieutenant Jim Jones: Then, the next time they came up at us, they actually did penetrate the 1st Platoon. Ray left his position and actually came back in through the lines to join the command group. Then we reconsolidated the 1st Platoon's lines to essentially cut the top of the ridgeline in half. Since they had gotten onto the ridgeline and if they would have turned to their right and attacked along that, we would have some defensive line.

Corporal Dave Smith: The most I can remember was an order saying 'Pull 1st Platoon back! Pull them back!' And that west end of the hill, we'd given up. The west end of the hill was all NVA.

Gunnery Sergeant Ralph Larsen: I didn't see a penetration. I just heard about the penetration, and I didn't even know about it because from where I was I couldn't see. All I knew was all these RPGs were flying around. I never saw so many RPGs blasting as I did that night. Seemed like half the people in the assault had RPGs. It was pretty bad, and of course I felt a little uncomfortable because I didn't have a hole. I did have a hole to lay in, but at the time we were going to have an attack, I moved in closer to the CP, just in case. Who knows they might say, 'Hey, do this.'

10 CONFUSION AND DEATH IN THE DARKNESS

The action continued to rage with most Marines firing desperately to their front, totally focused on their own small part of the battle. Most of them had no radio contact with anyone and little idea what was happening elsewhere on the ridge. While there were four radios per platoon (one for the Platoon Commander and one for each of the three squads), this translated to perhaps one radio for every four or five holes. Even in those foxholes where there was a radio, the Marine who operated it was generally preoccupied firing his weapon and throwing his grenades. Because of the deafening roar of the battle, it was necessary to squat down in the hole with the handset held hard against one ear, while the other hand was pressed against the other ear, trying to block out the noise. So confusion, predictably, reigned. Individual Marines were forced to rely solely on their training, their judgment, and their trust in each other.

THE SOUTHERN SLOPE (away from Route 9)

PFC Braden was at the extreme western end of 3rd Platoon's position, very near that point where they linked in with 1st Platoon's defense of the western finger. In his foxhole were two other Marines, one armed with an M-16 and the other armed only with a .45 caliber pistol, which contributed little to their firepower. Knowing this, the pistol-armed Marine was assigned to keep an eye out behind them and conserve his handful of bullets for any last-ditch stand.

PFC Dale Braden: I was still in the hole when they gave the word to fall back, but we didn't get the word. We had a guy in the hole with us, a radio man, but he didn't have a radio that night. He got into our hole with the two of us after the firefight started, and all he had was a .45. When we got opened up on, me and this other guy would jump up and fire. The guy with the .45 started firing behind us, and we thought he was shooting our own people. Then Lieutenant Dito come running down telling us that we were falling back. This kid jumped up out of the hole and took off running and got hit in both legs and then me and [the other Marine] jumped up and took off. When we went by, he just raised his arms up and we drug him that little part of the hill to where the CP was and to a corpsman.

THE WESTERN FINGER

Unknown to PFC Kinsella, Lance Corporal Walker and the other two Marines had climbed back into their mortar position after the enemy grenade had exploded in it. They soon took their first casualty.

Lance Corporal Alan "Chief" Walker: Then Horne got hit. So Gil and I are there and I said, 'Shit, man what are we going to do?' We were out of bullets. We were out of grenades. We were out of everything. I did save one grenade for the mortar tube. I thought, 'If nothing else I'm not going to have them sons of bitches use it on us.' So I blew the mortar up. I blew up my own mortar before I left. Before I pulled back, I dropped a grenade down into the firing pin.

Lance Corporal Walker and the two other Marines fell back, working their way cautiously across the narrow ridgeline in the area of the cleared landing zone. They made it to the north side, only to discover that the holes there had already been vacated. They continued on past them, down the northern slope, and then worked their way a few meters eastward before climbing back onto the ridge and attempting to rejoin Foxtrot.

Lance Corporal Alan "Chief" Walker: So we grabbed Horne and we just went over the top of the hill. Once we got going at a very low drag, low crawl on hands and knees, here come a whole bunch of gooks. We just plop down on the ground and laid there. And man, they was just like all around us. If we'd have sneezed or coughed, they'd have got us. When they pushed on, we started dragging Horne further up the hill. Here comes some more, and we just do the same thing. We don't even breathe. They was just talking and getting ready to charge up the hill, further up the hill. It was kind of amazing, but when we did make it over the crest of the hill, down on the side of the hill towards Route 9, there wasn't much going on over there at all.

So we made it on down to where the perimeter was, still inside the LZ. I can't remember what team was over there, but anyway we told them what happened. We got them guys and we pulled back, back around the side of the hill. And that's how we got back inside the perimeter. I didn't know they'd cut us off the perimeter. If we'd have charged up there, we probably would have been killed too. In fact, when we crawled around the back side of that hill, some Marines started shooting at us, and I told them, 'I'm Chief. I'm with 60 mortars.' And they knew who I was and they let us through.

Corporal Lockley, still lying in the half-filled trash pit at the far end of the finger, kept a close eye on the two new men in front of him. One of them had the squad radio. Then Corporal Lockley heard sounds behind him, which brought him momentary satisfaction, but that moment soon passed.

Corporal Ron "Pappy" Lockley: But anyway they had the radio in there and so I was right behind them. I mean I was close enough I could reach right out and touch them. We were that close. I heard some Vietnamese talking back behind me. Between us and where our CP was—where the lieutenant and all was— was some of that grass; it was about waist high, so I couldn't see over there. But I could hear them talking and I thought, 'Well, all right. We've captured some of them. That's good.' Well, it was just minutes later that it

sounded like 30 or more of them back behind us, and I
thought, 'No, that don't sound right.' So I told them,
my radio guy, whoever it was, I said, 'Hey, get on that
radio and find out what's going on. We got a bunch of
Vietnamese right behind us.' I told him to squat down
in the hole, you know, so he could talk and hear. And
when he squatted down in the hole, well the other guy
just squatted down in there with him. I kept trying to
get their attention, you know to say, 'Hey, somebody's
got to watch. You can't just hunker down in the hole
there.' As I did, one of the NVA just raised up right over
their hole with a grenade in his hand, up in the air, and
I popped him three times in the chest. Then my radio
man raised up out of the hole and he said, 'Hey, they've
pulled back. They've set up a new perimeter and they
say we're on our own.' So I knew there were at least 30
NVA behind us. There was a kind of a rise from where
we were, and if you walked back up the ridge you
know there was a rise and then it leveled off again. I
understand that's where they pulled the perimeter back
to. It was a pretty good ways. A pretty good distance.

Corporal Lockley had to make a quick decision. There
seemed little hope of fighting their way through the scores of
NVA soldiers behind them. Charging through them into the
Marines' lines also put them at grave risk of being killed by
their own men in the confusion.

Corporal Ron "Pappy" Lockley: I had to make a quick
decision. I said, 'Well, you know we'd have to fight our
way back to the perimeter.' So we decided to just go
ahead and bail off the hill there. We really had no idea
what the setup was behind us. Bad communications.
May have been on the part of this new guy who was
my radio man. I don't know, never did know.

The three of them rolled off the hill, planning to work their
towards Route 9 and the safety of LZ Hawk.
Confusion reigned. Many of the Marines could hardly
hear, their eardrums ringing from the concussion of countless
blasts of grenades and explosions and the muzzle blast of nearby rifles firing.

To the right of the now-empty mortar position on the south facing part of the finger, was the rocket team which included Lance Corporal Luebers and PFC Jacebo. Lance Corporal Luebers glanced to his left, and in the momentary light of a flare, saw a half-dozen or more NVA soldiers standing over the mortar position. Lance Corporal Luebers exclaimed, "Oh my God! They've got Chief," and sprinted over to his friend's rescue, killing the NVA soldiers with his M-16. But he was soon out of ammunition and was himself being pursued by other NVA soldiers. Lance Corporal Luebers ran back to his own position and hurriedly pushed his two comrades into the hole before diving in on top of them. The NVA soldiers were right behind him. Some used their bayonets on him, while others fired long bursts of fire into his body with their assault rifles.

COMMAND POST

At the command post, Corporal Smith would hear a sound he would never forget, although in the darkness and confusion of the night, he didn't know its source.

Corporal Dave Smith: Then I remember hearing someone. It sounded like someone was being bayoneted because I can remember that scream. I still can't forget that. I don't know who it was, but it was someone on the south side of the ridge, probably someone in 1st Platoon.

Lance Corporal Walker eventually made it safely back into the Foxtrot perimeter. He did so by the circuitous route of climbing down the northern slope, moving along the base of the ridge to the east, and then climbing back up again. He then proceeded to the CP to tell Lieutenant Jones what he had seen.

Lance Corporal Alan "Chief" Walker: By the time we pulled back, they'd already set up a new perimeter. If we'd have charged up there, we probably would have been killed too. In fact, when we crawled around the back side of that hill, some Marines started shooting at us. I told them, 'I'm Chief. I'm with 60 mortars.' And they knew who I was and they let us through. I remember walking through. One of the first people I saw was Dickie Cutbirth, and I ask him where the CO is and he tells me where he's at.

I remember talking with Jones and I told him, 'Well, the gooks are inside the LZ. I don't know how many Marines are alive down there, but if they are, they probably won't be living long.' He said, 'I'm going to bomb the LZ,' and I said, 'They're gathering down there now. They're getting ready to attack you.'

1st Lieutenant Jim Jones: They essentially got up there and didn't know what to do once they got up on top. So that gave us a good opportunity to take a lot of them out and broke the attack on the top of the ridgeline. The ones who were left got into the holes that 1st Platoon had vacated and essentially stayed there until we drove them off one way or the other.

11 | CHAOS AND TERROR

There were a frantic few minutes of utter confusion while most of the survivors of 1st Platoon pulled back and attempted to regroup. It soon became clear that not everyone down there was aware of it, and worse, in some of the positions overrun by the NVA, wounded Marines might still remain.

THE WESTERN FINGER

Sergeant McCoy enlisted the help of PFC Rodriquez, and the two of them crept back down past the LZ and onto the finger. They witnessed a scene of madness and chaos in 1st Platoon's old positions down on the western finger. NVA soldiers were running back and forth across the ridge while others stood milling around. Still others went in search of wounded Marines.

Sergeant Dave McCoy: Chico didn't want to go down there and I told him, I said, 'There's guys down there who have got to be alive.' There was still shooting going on. 'We've got to go down there.' He said, 'Oh, man!' I said, 'Come on. We'll just stay on this side here.' So we moved on down and we went from hole to hole.

Basically we could see them down there. They were shooting in the holes. I didn't personally see a North Vietnamese, you know, make an American kneel and shoot him in the back of the head. I didn't see that, but

I do know that if an American was laying there, they were shooting him and not with just one shot: They were putting three or four rounds into him. Chico and I, we made probably six or seven trips down there. It seemed like a long, long time. I know whenever we saw two or three North Vietnamese together, if we didn't have a really good shot at them, we wouldn't. We'd just stayed down. When they'd run over to another hole, we'd move along further. Then if we got a good shot at them, we'd shoot those three, but it'd seem like there'd be two or three more who would pop up somewhere else. Then they'd start shooting at us, and we'd get down and haul ass back. Pretty soon we'd head back out again. I don't know if they were doing it, but it sounded like, you know, Americans down there, you know, looking for help. There was a lot of moaning and a lot of pain down there that night.

First Platoon's medical corpsman, 20-year-old Hospitalman 2nd Class (HM2) Frank "Doc" Sarwicki, was cut off from the main body when 1st Platoon was overrun. He was busy ministering to several badly wounded Marines who lay on the ground around him. He kept them alive for several long minutes. Eventually, though, one of his patients moaned from his pain and the NVA heard it. The NVA then approached and, at point-blank range, killed each of the Marines with a bullet to the head. They thought they had done the same to "Doc" Sarwicki. However, the bullet penetrated his steel helmet and ricocheted downward off the helmet's fiberglass liner, thus knocking him unconscious but only causing a superficial wound to his face.

Sergeant McCoy continued on his mission to rescue wounded Marines, risking his own life in the process.

Sergeant Dave McCoy: I was down in a hole trying to get a guy out; he was breathing. I set my rifle down on the side of the hole and here comes 'smiley' right up in front of the hole. He was ready to blow me away. Chico cut him down, just like that. They were already there. The North Vietnamese had thrown satchel charges all over the top of that hill. I think they had went around and randomly shot in holes, because they were running from one side to the other. When we were down there, Chico and I, they were all over the place. They were running across the hill and going down the other side. It was crazy. They would come up shooting, and then they would run all the way—it wasn't that wide of a hill there—completely over the top of it until they were at the other side. Then they'd figure, 'Well I messed up, I've got to stay up here.' They evidently thought it was wider than that, too. They made it from the holes on the north side to the south side in probably less than 15 seconds. They were across the whole thing. The North Vietnamese were all over 1st Platoon's positions.

Having personally informed Lieutenant Jones about the situation down on the finger, Lieutenant Dito crawled back toward that area, moving from hole to hole along the southern side of the ridge. When he got to what was clearly the last remaining group of Marines along that side (one of whom was PFC Bruce Holt), he told them of their situation.

2nd Lieutenant Ray Dito: I think I got to Holt. I think he was in one of the other platoons. He had a round face, a couple of scars. He was a real tough customer. He had been there since I joined the platoon. He was on the other side of the mortars to the left near the Crow's Nest. I told Holt, 'This is where we're going to stay. Right here. Because they're between us and the end of the finger.' So I was staying there with Holt, and then I was back over with Tex. I kind of worked this little triangle from there back up to wherever Jones was situated, and I'd let him know what was going on. Then I'd go back down to the lines and stay down there and check on things. I never had a radio the rest of the night.

With PFC Holt on the left and Corporal La Bonte on the right, other Marines formed a line linking the two and sealing the NVA from moving westward toward the rest of Foxtrot. One of the Marines joining this line was PFC Kinsella, having taken the wounded Marine to the corpsman for medical assistance.

PFC Dave Kinsella: I left him there with the corpsman and then went back to, basically, where I was, where we started out. I was set up in a line with these guys across the ridge there. That's where I spent the rest of the night. I think somebody said something about forming a line, you know. We were basically just laying in the grass, and I remember the artillery. You could just hear the big chunks of shrapnel flying through the air. When I left out of my hole, I didn't even have any ammunition. My rifle was the only thing I had. When I got to the other side, I got some magazines from somebody in the hole that was right there.

Other Marines, drawn from the less heavily engaged northern slope, helped out on this critically important new defensive line. One of them was Lance Corporal Curtis "Snake" Clark, who had celebrated his 18th birthday only two months ago and who now took up a position alongside PFC Kinsella. Lance Corporal Clark, of Memphis, Tennessee, had joined the Marines at the age of 17 at the insistence of his mother, who was con-

Lance Corporal Curtis "Snake" Clark and another Marine about to move out again on another patrol in early May 1968. (Credit: Curtis Clark)

cerned about the "bad company" he was keeping. "She told me I was either going to join the Marines or go to jail."

Lance Corporal Curtis "Snake" Clark: It was very grassy and you couldn't see in front of you. The line was very thin. I couldn't see who was to the left or to the right of me. They issued us with extra hand grenades and, because the line was so thin, naturally we didn't want to fire. So any movement we heard, we threw grenades at. We pretty much just stayed there and tossed grenades.

THE CROW'S NEST

The battle continued to rage at the vital Crow's Nest position as well. Most of the Marines there had no accurate picture of the whole battle. The events occurring down on the ridge, especially for those like PFC Gentry whose position faced away from the company, remained clouded in mystery.

PFC Chris Gentry: We didn't have a whole lot of radio contact the entire night. I think the one radio we had, Harold kept it on the 'call for fire' frequency. I don't think we ever talked to the company the whole night.

We got an awful lot of incoming grenades. You could see the sparks coming off the ChiCom as it was coming in. I think everybody was probably throwing ChiComs back. You know, they'd land with a 'thump.' We'd pick it up and throw it back, hoping it didn't go off.

12 THE MARINES REGROUP AND HOLD

By 4:00 AM the battle had been raging for over an hour. The entire perimeter of Foxtrot's defenses was being assaulted by massed waves of NVA soldiers. Meanwhile, the Marines were also undergoing a steady barrage of RPGs. The western end of the perimeter, the finger area, had been ceded to the NVA. The Marines now formed a new line cutting off that area from the enemy. It was estimated that there were 60 or more NVA soldiers milling about in 1st Platoon's area. Witnesses described them as ". . . babbling incoherently, yelling, laughing, screaming, smoking, anything you might imagine." It seems clear that they must have believed they had won the battle and were unaware that the Marines had simply reconsolidated nearby. Within moments, the laughing NVA were struck down by an avalanche of artillery and mortars directed onto them by the Marines.

THE COMMAND POST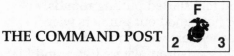

Having been advised that NVA troops were now on the western finger of the ridge, the area once occupied by 1st Platoon, Lieutenant Jones directed hitting the area with artillery and mortars.

1st Lieutenant Jim Jones: I do remember making a decision and telling the FO to walk the artillery in, and when he said, 'We're already at 75 meters,' I said,

'Bring it in to 25 meters.' Then I called all the platoons and told people to get down in their holes because it was essentially going to come down on top of us. By sheer luck and the skill of the artillery guys, the north-ernmost rounds impacted just really outside our lines. The artillery was just a steel curtain. I remember once we thought we had a lull in the action and I ordered a ceasefire. The troops started screaming, 'Here they come again,' and then we started firing again and that broke up the attack. I remember the voices from the lines, saying, 'Don't stop. Don't stop. They're coming!'

The 81-mm mortar platoon also added its deadly firepower to Foxtrot's defenses, controlled by Corporal Smith, having now moved back further away from the western finger area.

Corporal Dave Smith: When things really started happening, when 1st Platoon had to pull back, me and my radio man had to pull back too because we were at the edge of where the new perimeter was going to be. So when we pulled back, we didn't have a hole or anything and we just lay there. When I pulled back, Jones was right between four to five yards of me then. We're not talking massive distances here.

I started putting in rounds all around that end of the ridge. And by the end of the night I was putting them in on the south side. After 1st Platoon pulled back—I can't remember if it was Lieutenant Jones or Gunny Larsen—said, 'Hey we need them closer.' Because the NVA were up where 1st Platoon had been. The NVA were up on top of the ridge. I started putting rounds down there. I remember how good our gunners were back at the platoon because there were some rounds that were coming in at 20 yards from where I was, and I was always concerned. I said, 'Hey, there's guys still down there.' The response was: 'No. No ones down there that you have to worry about.'

My main memories are of being confused, being scared. I was a little out-of-it at times with my fever. At some point I was just laying out flat on the ground and there's this big stinking explosion at my feet. What had happened was that an RPG went off right at my feet but

I didn't get a scratch. The RPG had buried itself in the ground before it went off. My radio man got shot in the butt and it creased one of his cheeks, literally tore him a new asshole. It wasn't a deep wound, just a grazing wound, but it opened up one of his cheeks.

Gunny Larsen was one of the real heroes there, him being there and being so self-assured, kept others going. It was like we all fed off each other's courage. He was one of the unsung heroes there. He was a rock.

Gunnery Sergeant Ralph Larsen: It's amazing after a heavy artillery or mortar barrage and you say, 'How the devil did we get through this?' If you're in a little bit of defilade, of course, and it hits close, it's going to miss you. It's going to screw up your hearing and all that but, you know, bursts go 'up and away,' especially when you see all those RPGs going off. That's a colorful thing. It's like some kind of fireworks-type thing. It's more concussion than anything else.

I thought the guys were doing a pretty good job. They were putting out a good volume of fire from around where I could see. I didn't see anybody who was having a problem. This is the one thing I do remember telling people: 'Stay in your holes!! Don't get up and run around!! Stay in your holes.' That'll get people killed quicker than anything I know.

THE EASTERN END (facing the Crow's Nest)

The shooting and the incoming RPGs and grenades were relentless. Red tracers from Marine weapons zipped out into the darkness and occasionally ricocheted wildly into the sky when they hit a rock or other hard surface. Meanwhile, green tracers from NVA weapons zoomed in out of the darkness, impacting on the ridge and all around the Marines. Every time an RPG impacted, it did so not only with a shuddering explosion that seemed to rip the air, but also with a blinding flash of light that temporarily blinded the vision like a flashbulb going off in the face. Every few minutes an illumination round would pop to life in the sky hundreds of yards overhead and descend by parachute, the flare burning so intensely that it lit up the ridge like some sort of ghostly moonscape. The flares burned so brightly, like a welder's arc, that the Marines had to shield their eyes from the glare. Meanwhile, as the flares descended, they swayed back and forth like a pendulum from the parachute they were attached to, causing the harsh shadows thus created to dance and move in time to the descent. The shadows would lengthen as the flare came closer and closer to the ground and then suddenly there would be nothing but darkness. All of this took place to the constant roar of gunfire and explosions.

PFC Kevin Henry: My memory in general is that I see tracers going off everywhere. I remember the night illumination coming down, and I knew something bad was going to happen. I mean, I knew we were really in the shit. I reached a certain point in my mind where I really didn't believe that we were going to live to see the sun come up.

PFC Mark Woodruff: For quite a while, I was in the same hole with Sergeant Quinn. He kind of made his rounds checking up on everybody and for some reason kind of settled in with me for quite a while. He was good. We were both crouching down into the hole to avoid all the shrapnel and the bullets that were flying all over the place. Every so often, he sort of jumped up, popped up out of the hole and let rip with his M-16, kind of like hosing down the area to our front and also to our right a little bit.

Sergeant Joseph Quinn: Then we were shooting. You're up, you're down. You're up, you're down. We all had fields of fire. You couldn't shoot too high because then you'd be firing into the positions in front of you. The Crow's Nest was above us and in front of us.

PFC Woodruff was armed with the 3.5-inch rocket launcher, introduced during the Korean War to replace the World War II "bazooka." It was essentially a hollow tube with an electrical magneto in the trigger. When the trigger was squeezed, an electrical charge fired the nine-pound rocket. When he'd first fired it back in training at Camp Pendleton, he'd been amazed that it wasn't at all like in the movies. In the movies, a bazooka always fired with a *whishhhing* sound, like a Fourth of July sky-rocket. In reality, he discovered it fired with a quick, short, sharp boom. He would learn that the rocket only burned for a fraction of a second, and by the time it left the five-foot-long tube, it was entirely burned out and flew the entire distance to the target by momentum in freeflight. He also learned about the dangerous "backblast" area, extending to a distance of about 25 yards behind the launcher where gasses and flames coming out of the rocket could cause injury. And it was also drummed into him throughout his training that, because of this backblast of flame, the 3.5-inch rocket launcher should never be fired at night. The fireball coming out of the back would immediately give away the shooter's position and attract enemy fire.

PFC Mark Woodruff: I wasn't doing a whole lot to help out. I remember Quinn looking at the launcher next to the hole and asking, 'What else have you got?' When I pointed to my four grenades and showed him my pistol and two spare magazines—fifteen rounds in all—I could see the disappointment on his face. It was about that time that I saw him mumble a prayer and I knew this was serious.

Because the terrain dipped away to their front, most of the "saddle" area remained in shadow, even when flares or illumination rounds provided vision in other areas.

PFC Mark Woodruff: Then later on—and I have no idea how much later this is—somebody came over to the hole, you know all crouched down and everything and said, you know kind of whispered, 'Woody, the Crow's Nest says there's a shitload of gooks in the saddle in front of us and they want you to put some rockets out there.' I'm not sure who that was but it might have been Dickie Cutbirth, maybe Skip Hedrick. I was really in a dilemma there for a couple of minutes. I mean I was scared out of my mind and wasn't that happy about firing the thing, but mainly I was worried about doing the wrong thing. You know, like someone's going to yell at me, 'What the hell do you think you're doing! Didn't they teach you anything in training?'

Anyway, eventually I thought, 'What the hell,' and looked behind me to make sure nobody was in the backblast area and fired a round into that bomb crater in front of us about 30 or 40 yards away. I knew if there were gooks out there, that's where they'd be. It was dark of course and I couldn't see it, but I had memorized its location in the last few days and the 3.5-inch launcher was long enough that, even though the sights were no good at night, you could just point it pretty accurately. So it went *kaboom* and a few seconds later my rocket hit out in front with another *kaboom*. By then I was already crouching back down in the hole by the time it hit. And nobody yelled at me and nobody said anything so I continued to fire from time to time, mainly into the saddle but I put a few rounds onto the southern slope leading up to the Crow's Nest too.

Sergeant Joseph Quinn: Woody was firing there and then they would return fire to wherever he was. They were trying to hit him. Unluckily, I was in the same hole as him. I remember reaching up one time to get another magazine. I had it on the edge of the hole, and I just reached up and, that fast, a round hit that magazine and I quick jerked my hand back. It missed me, but they must have been right in front of us waiting for him; they might have thought it was a head or something. I remember that my whole life: that damned guy in the hole with me shooting his damned bazooka. Christ! I'm trying to be quiet and hide and he's saying, 'Hey, Over here! *Boom*!' Look at us! Over here! *Boom*! We'll draw their fire. *Boom*!!' He had the bazooka. I didn't like him a whole lot that night. They were really going crazy over him! They were trying to shoot him.

Up in the Crow's Nest, the Marines were aware that the NVA had occupied that "saddle" area between themselves and the company position. They were glad for any help they could get and happily observed PFC Woodruff's actions.

PFC Mike Nichols: There were gooks in the saddle. There were, all kinds of them. I can remember Woody firing down there. I remember seeing it. I think Chris and all those boys could, too. It would light up, you know. It was wild looking: the backblast.

Lance Corporal Doug "Deuce" Near: Somewhere along the line there shortly—I don't know how long into the battle—the word got passed down the line to fix bayonets. It dawned on me then, like, this is something you read in a book. You know, fix bayonets. Never in my wildest dreams did I ever think that— well, I didn't have a bayonet, I had a damned Kabar [Marine Corps fighting knife]. But I just put that in the ground in front of me and then the word was passed that anybody outside the foxhole was considered to be the enemy. Shoot anything that moved. You could see the tracers and you could hear like a whistle. It must have been to either retreat or to keep on charging. And they just kept coming.

And I thought, 'I'm not going home. I'm not walking home. I'm going to be dead tonight.' I thought for sure that I was going to die that night. I really thought that was the end for me that night. We were going to go down fighting as hard as we could and whatever happened, happened.

PFC Kevin Henry: Dickie was up and down the lines checking everybody out. And I remember seeing him briefly going back and forth. The most memory I have is that our visions were so narrowly focused; we didn't have a broad vision of anything. We were more concerned with what was going on in front of our own position. There was no way I was going to give up my hole, and there was no way you were going to give up your hole. If they come, they come. I'm ready.

THE CROW'S NEST

The Crow's Nest continued to be under heavy attack itself while also providing a frightening view of the action on the ridge below.

PFC Harold Blunk: All I had to do was look to the right and I'm looking at the ridge, and I still had a clear view looking south, opposite Route 9. If you look at a map, there's a ridgeline about 700 meters that is as high as the Crow's Nest if not a little higher, and I believe that's where they were firing the RPGs from. Because when we looked down at Foxtrot Ridge, it was like the Fourth of July down there. For them to have RPG rounds in what appeared to me to be airbursts blowing up right inside the perimeter of Foxtrot Ridge. I saw all those explosions down there and thought, 'These guys are all dead down there. There's no way anyone can live through that. I was feeling that we [on the Crow's Nest] were lucky because at least they weren't over us, firing down at you. Lobbing them in like they were onto the ridge.

The NVA apparently didn't realize that the Crow's Nest was so small and manned by so few Marines. Often, they crept up and threw their "ChiCom" grenades with a mighty heave, only to have the grenades sail over the Marines' position and land instead on the opposite slope, sometimes amid their own troops attacking from that other side.

PFC Robert "Hillbilly" Croft: They threw a lot of ChiComs. Then it was such a small perimeter right there, they overthrew a lot of them, too. That helped us.

PFC Chris Gentry: I used up all my grenades first; I liked those as an area weapon. Then just every minute or so, I'd just hold my M-16 down and spray 20 rounds of full automatic across the front of us. And that's how my firefight went that night. Larry was doing the same thing until he was killed. I thought if I could kill them real quick, they would have less opportunity to kill me. And I really did not want to be killed. So I didn't mind shooting it up. I had grown up—being born and raised in Alaska—I was in the woods all the time with a rifle in my hands, so it was not unusual circumstances. But I was not used to the 'game' shooting back.

LZ HAWK

Lieutenant Tehan, back at LZ Hawk, was in the ideal position to witness Foxtrot's artillery and mortar batteries at work. He noted that nearby Khe Sanh also added its artillery support to Foxtrot. Because of the terrain and the lay of the land, their artillery was actually better placed to provide effective support.

2nd Lieutenant William Tehan: Most of Foxtrot's artillery that night came from Khe Sanh. The guns at Khe Sanh were to Foxtrot's northwest and so they could reach the south side of the hill, whereas Bravo couldn't shoot on the south side of the hill. Also, the guns at Khe Sanh could shoot to the west side where the ridge tapered off going down toward Khe Sanh village. They had a better angle of fire shooting into the ridge on the northwest side. Most of the artillery coming in was coming in from Khe Sanh—the 105s at Khe Sanh. Bravo 1/12 did fire also, but I remember that Colonel Davis was concerned the weapons we had at LZ Hawk couldn't cover where Jim was trying to get the fire to go.

13 | THE NVA ASSAULT CONTINUES UNABATED

By now it was about 4:30 AM with sunrise a good two hours away. The NVA continued their attack relentlessly without letting up.

THE SOUTHERN SLOPE (away from Route 9)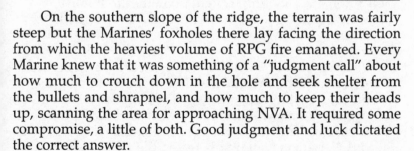

On the southern slope of the ridge, the terrain was fairly steep but the Marines' foxholes there lay facing the direction from which the heaviest volume of RPG fire emanated. Every Marine knew that it was something of a "judgment call" about how much to crouch down in the hole and seek shelter from the bullets and shrapnel, and how much to keep their heads up, scanning the area for approaching NVA. It required some compromise, a little of both. Good judgment and luck dictated the correct answer.

Lance Corporal Robert Kincaid: As that fire intensified toward the hole, we just kind of crouched down in the hole, stopped firing and kinda like pulled the hole in over top of us. We just got down in there; I remember hearing Vietnamese speaking. I could hear them talking from directly in front of us. I knew we couldn't get the gun up, and I can remember my teeth were chattering so loud that I thought they could hear me. My knees were really weak. I was crouched there, sitting on my butt with my knees pulled up to my chin. The hole to

my left had a fellow by the name of Mylin in it, Steve
Mylin. He was in the hole direct to my left, and I heard
him yell out, 'We're overran.'

What Lance Corporal Kinkaid had actually heard, no
doubt garbled and nearly drowned out by the din of the battle,
was Lance Corporal Mylin's exhortation for someone to shoot
an NVA soldier who had managed to creep up upon them.

Lance Corporal Steve Mylin: A gook actually came
right up to our fighting hole. We were down, hunkered
down, shit was flying in so bad. All three of us were
hunkered down. This gook snuck right up. He was
crawling but his head—I can remember there was a
light from a flare or something that lit him up—and I
remember seeing his face and the camouflage around
his helmet. And this gook—I remember it just like it
was yesterday—he had camouflage on his helmet and I
tried shooting him with my M-16 and it jammed. One
of the guys from my team had an M-14 and I yelled,
'Shoot that gook! Shoot that gook!' He just opened up
on automatic shooting straight up in the air. It must
have scared the gook, but whatever it did he turned
and ran.

Whether the NVA soldier was grazed by a bullet, temporarily stunned by the muzzle blast of the M-14 only inches
from his face, or simply frightened, he disappeared back down
the slope. Fortunately, the scream had caused Lance Corporal
Kinkaid to raise his head up out of his foxhole and sight two
other NVA soldiers standing between the two holes, looking
back downhill. Then the burst of gunfire caught the attention
of the two NVA soldiers, and they turned to face Lance
Corporal Mylin, about to fire in his direction.

Lance Corporal Robert Kincaid: When Mylin yelled
that, 'We're overran,' I stuck my head up. When I stuck
my head up, there were two North Vietnamese soldiers
standing with their back at our hole and they were
looking downhill, like they didn't see our hole or know
that we were there. I was shaking to death. I remember
and I'm not a bit ashamed to say that I was scared to

death. When I looked, those two Vietnamese soldiers standing there had faced Mylin's direction and the corporal that was with me shot one with his M-16, and I shot the other one with the shotgun.

It was kind of a simultaneous. I mean we didn't plan, we didn't conspire to shoot these people. It was just like a conditioned reflex. And I didn't really pick which one. I just shot the one that was closest to me. That was the one to my right. I had double-ought buck in that shotgun. Double-ought buck, and he went down.

Then it really intensified. Heavy small arms fire. It got loud. I could hear voices. I could hear yelling. I could hear screaming. And RPGs kept pouring in. I remember RPGs throwing dirt in the hole on top of us. I can remember the dirt going down the back of my T-shirt. And then I can remember it was just Charlie Kohler and myself in the hole. I don't know where the other guy went.

Lance Corporal Steve Mylin: I don't know how anyone else felt that night, but there was no doubt in my mind that I wasn't going to make it. At one point I had a hand grenade in each hand with the pins pulled. That's how sure I was that we were going to get overrun.

THE CROW'S NEST

PFC Croft continued to put out a steady fire with his M-60 machine gun. Despite the hail of incoming bullets, he blazed away at the attackers nonstop. He knew that the M-60 has a "cyclic" rate of fire of 550 rounds per minute. In theory, that's how many bullets it could fire in one minute if the gunner kept his finger on the trigger and the assistant-gunner kept feeding it ammunition. But PFC Croft knew that it's only theoretical because, in fact, the heat thus generated would quickly burn out the barrel and the weapon would seize up just like an overheated car. So instead, machine gunners are rigidly trained to fire in short, four-to-six round bursts, pausing for a second or two before doing so again (*ta-ta-ta-ta*, pause, *ta-ta-ta-ta*, pause, *ta-ta-ta-ta*) in order to allow the gun to cool off. PFC Croft discovered that even this is only theoretical, concluding that

there's not much sense in saving the gun at the cost of the
Marine firing it.

PFC Robert "Hillbilly" Croft: And then I burned the
machine gun up. Had to. That four-to-six round burst is
good if you only have four-to-six gooks coming at a
time. But when you got a whole bunch of them. . . .
Actually Mouse said he saw that the barrel was so hot
that the piston under the barrel, he saw that thing go
back and forth that night.

The Marines still had some ammunition for the now inoperable machine gun. The machine gun, however, fired a 7.62-
mm round, which could not be used in the 5.56-mm M-16 rifles
carried by most Marines. Fortunately, one of the Marines on
the Crow's Nest had recently swapped rifles and acquired an
M-14. The M-16 had a reputation for jamming. Foxtrot had
retained ten or so of the more reliable M-14s in their inventory.
Best of all for the Marines on the Crow's Nest, it fired the same
7.62-mm ammunition as the M-60 machine gun.

PFC Robert "Hillbilly" Croft: But luckily, there was an
M-14 up there. Howell might have brought it up there, I
don't know. So, after that, I got the M-14. I had the rest
of the M-60 ammo, had them unlink it and load it in the
M-14 magazines, so I could use it.

Corporal Kevin "Canadian" Howell: There was two
gullies running up, towards the Crow's Nest and the
Crow's Nest overlooked the company area. They were
trying to get up there. They knew, as well as everybody
else did, that the key to that feature was to take out the
Crow's Nest because then they could bring fire down
onto the company. They would try coming up the gullies on the left and right, and we would go over and lie
there and throw rocks because we were short on ammo.
If we heard the rocks hit rocks, we knew we were okay.
If we didn't hear the rocks hit, we followed up with a
hand grenade.
    I was to the left of Hillbilly and Mouse's machine gun.
We had our back to the company, basically. So I would
have to go left and right to where those two gullies

were during the night to try and prevent these guys from coming up through the gullies. You know, throw rocks, move over to the other one and throw rocks, and stuff like that.

PFC Mike Nichols: I remember those ChiComs, they were throwing them. They were so close we could see them spark when they would pull the cord on them. You know how they would spark. We could see them spark. They were that close to us. They'd throw them and, well, they were going off just every now and then, all around. But you know how those things were; they'd pretty much blow over you.

Corporal Kevin "Canadian" Howell: That's what you saw all night. Everything was sparks. It was trails and sparks and flares and stuff. When we went down to pick up their weapons, we purposely didn't pick up their hand grenades because they were worthless. They were mostly a shock grenade, a tin can with an explosive in it. And they were unsteady.

PFC Mike Nichols: Anyway, I remember those ChiComs. Those gooks, you know, we could hear them a talking and jabbering and going on. They were just right down in under the top of the hill from us.

The Marines on the Crow's Nest, uncertain about how many Marines remained alive on the ridge below, began saying "goodbye" to one another, believing themselves to be overrun and killed at any moment.

PFC Robert "Hillbilly" Croft: And when it got real bad, it was one of those, 'Well, it was nice knowing you,' kind of discussions. 'We've had it.' I forget the exact phrase, but at that point, well, the action had been going on for a little bit, and then we were running out of ammunition and we figured that was pretty much it. We had nowhere to go. And the company, it didn't sound any better down there. So we figured we'd just stand our ground.

THE COMMAND POST

Having spoken to Lieutenant Jones, Lance Corporal Walker joined the other mortar team that was near the CP. An RPG hit nearby and knocked him to ground and sent his eyeglasses flying.

Lance Corporal Alan "Chief" Walker: I got wounded shortly after I talked to Jones. Dickie Cutbirth was one of the second or third guys that came up to me and wanted to know if I was all right. My glasses was gone and I knew I got hit. And it was either him or someone who found them. I said, 'How in the hell did they find my glasses in the middle of the night?' But he wanted to know how I was doing. And I said, 'God, I guess I'm okay.' And he said, 'Well, all your arms and legs are there,' and so I said, 'I guess that's okay.' I remember he ran off with ammo. I could see the machine gun ammo.

Corporal Dave Smith: I'd pop my head up once in a while—not too much—and I'd spot my flashes. You know, once you're around 81s and artillery so much, you know the difference between what 105 rounds are like and what my [mortar] rounds are like. And I just kind of adjusted all night. I was coming in all around on the slopes coming up. You know when you set up every night, 81s and artillery, you have your night defenses and you set up a spotter round on every approach on every side. So I was just adjusting from them all over. I was just shooting everyplace I could find.

Gunnery Sergeant Ralph Larsen: You're not worrying about the weather or anything else. You're staring. Your eyes are wide because you're thinking, 'Jeez, I don't want to miss anything. You see somebody coming, you'd better get them before he gets you, you know.' And who is going to win Custer's Last Stand this time?

THE WESTERN FINGER

Marine mortars and artillery were now pounding the western end of the ridge and impacting only a few yards from the Marines who formed the new defensive line.

2nd Lieutenant Ray Dito: There were some mortars; I thought they were our mortars. They were impacting almost on top of us. I went back up to Jones and I said, 'You've got to tell them to check fire; they're dropping them right on top of us.' Well, I think that's what he intended.

One of the Marines who formed the defensive line was Corporal Baker, who had been shot in the right leg but managed to bandage his own wound with a battle dressing. He was now armed with an M-79 grenade launcher and fired grenades down onto the unsuspecting NVA soldiers below. The weapon was particularly effective against those NVA troops sheltering in 1st Platoon's old foxholes and thus shielded from rifle fire. At one point he rushed forward to aid another wounded Marine, dragging him to safety but was wounded again in the process. This wound would prove fatal, despite the attempts of other Marines to stem the bleeding.

2nd Lieutenant Ray Dito: A short time later Baker came over to me and he had been wounded seriously. I think his name was Steven Baker. He was a corporal; he was a squad leader. He was wounded and he was with me for a while, still alive at that point. I was with him, off and on, throughout the night. He must have died some time before sunup. Either he bled out or died of shock or something like that because I never saw him on his feet after he came to where I was. I know he got hit while he and I were laying side by side. Whether that was the wound that actually killed him, I don't know, but I know he was hit and we were 'butt-up' against each other.

THE NORTHERN SLOPE (facing Route 9)

Foxtrot's own 60-mm mortars continued to fire their few precious rounds sparingly. Sergeant Pressler directed these by standing on a vantage point on the northern slope and then running back to the mortars, a few meters behind him, to tell them where and when to fire. While sometimes the area was lit with flares, there were long periods of darkness, too, between the various 'illumination' missions. During those times, Sergeant Pressler simply called out to his mortar team and then followed their voices.

> **Sergeant Hubert "Dick" Pressler:** Just like, you know going back and forth to direct the fire. And I'd say, 'Sixty mike-mike? Sixty mike-mike?' And they'd say, 'Yeah, here! Yeah, here!' And then I'd tell them where to go and then I'd run back down and I kept going back and forth. Then one time I turn around and I say, 'Sixty mike-mike? Sixty mike-mike?' And then they say, 'Yeah, here,' and the next thing you know I say, 'Direct . . ." and *Blamm*! The next thing you know, there it was: the ChiComs came in. They came close enough that it knocked all of us off our feet. And then we got back up and started in again. But they were throwing at us because we must have been doing some type of damage. That was a time when I was really scared.

PFC Braden soon found himself manning a hole on this northern slope, only two holes to the left of 2nd Platoon and so almost back among his closest friends.

> **PFC Dale Braden:** I went across the ridge to the steep side, looking onto Route 9. I got into another hole with a guy from 3rd Platoon. That's where I stayed the rest of the night. And then I was back in the line with 2nd Platoon because my squad leader was just two holes over from me.
> There was an antiaircraft gun the gooks had down in a bomb crater and it pinned our whole side down for

just about the rest of the night. We'd just jump up every now and then and shoot.

THE EASTERN END (facing the Crow's Nest)

Lance Corporal Near carried one of Foxtrot's M-14s. He did so partially because of its reliability but also in order to use the tracer rounds easily available from the machine gunners. He could thus "spot" or identify targets for the 3.5-inch rocket launcher by firing a tracer round and telling the gunner, "Fire over there." In the darkness and confusion, he loaded a magazine into his weapon filled entirely with tracer ammunition.

Lance Corporal Doug "Deuce" Near: I was carrying an M-14 because I used to carry that for the spotter round for Woody. I don't know if the gooks got mixed up or what, but you know they were trying to take over that little knob, the Crow's Nest, so they would have had the high ground and would have just tore us a new asshole. There were some gooks that got between us and the knob and they were coming up and you could just see 'em, you know, the outline with the flares and stuff. I recall seeing one who had something strapped to his chest. He was coming directly to the foxhole off to my right somewhere, over where Dickie's machine gun was. He was coming up right in there so I assume he was after the gun team. I unloaded this 20 round tracer magazine into this gook and he exploded on us. He must have exploded, oh 20, 25 feet out but it didn't dawn on me at that time that he had a satchel charge attached to him or something. I saw him, unloaded on him and he exploded.

PFC Kevin Henry: Our vision was so focused because all you were concerned about was your field of fire in front of your hole, such as our holes were. They weren't very deep because the ground was rock hard. I don't think my hole was any deeper than knee deep, if that. I just said, 'Oh God. If I'm going to die I just don't want it to hurt too much.' I remember Woodruff and I remember Dickie Cutbirth was in the hole off to our

right. I remember Woodruff and I running around a little bit with our eyes wide open, just waiting for them to
come up.

LZ HAWK

One of the bunkers at LZ Hawk served as the command
post for the Battalion Commander, Colonel Davis. With him
were the dozen or so other Marines of his staff, huddled over
maps and speaking into radios. They monitored the course of
the battle Foxtrot was engaged in. One of the voices they
heard throughout the night was that of PFC Blunk, who continued to direct artillery fire onto the enemy using the battalion's own battery (Bravo 1/12) as well as Khe Sanh's artillery,
which had a better angle of fire onto the ridge and hence was
more vital.

PFC Harold Blunk: At one point in the battle the
artillery stopped completely. There was no more
artillery support. I was on the radio screaming for
more artillery. I later discovered that the artillery batteries were running on "danger low" on their supply
of artillery rounds and that's why they cut it off.

Lieutenant Tehan, still stranded at LZ Hawk, happened
to be in the CP bunker there with Colonel Davis when the
Khe Sanh batteries indicated their "danger low" ammunition
status. He recalls Colonel Davis's reaction, threatening to
order his own artillery (Bravo 1/12) to begin shelling Khe
Sanh.

2nd Lieutenant William Tehan: Well, I was in and out
of the CP bunker that night and at one point when Fox
was getting hit real heavy, right there in the middle of
the night, one of the artillery batteries at Khe Sanh
said they were going to stop firing because they were
low on ammunition. The people at Khe Sanh said,
'Hey, we're getting low on ammo. We're not going to
be able to keep this up.' And Davis just blew a cork. I
mean Davis went right through the overhead. He was
screaming and hollering on the radio. He went into

LZ Hawk. Its artillery and mortars fired in support of the Marines of Foxtrot 2/3. (Credit: Author's collection)

one of his two-minute profanities, and I thought he was going to have a stroke. And so he told them, 'If you stop shooting I'm going to start shooting at you with Bravo.' I don't think he was going to, but it added emphasis that he was serious about what was going on.

The artillery resumed and Foxtrot continued to receive the pinpoint accuracy of the Khe Sanh artillery battery as well as the support of their own Bravo Battery.

14 | THE SITUATION BECOMES INCREASINGLY DESPERATE

By 5:00 AM the battle continued unabated. The Marines' supporting arms, their mortars and artillery, formed a wall of death around the perimeter but the NVA continued to press forward. The Marines were amazed that so many NVA soldiers were able to survive that barrage and close with them to grenade and bayonet range. Equally, the Marines up on the Crow's Nest looked down at the Marines on the ridge and were amazed that any of them survived down there to continue the fight against the NVA.

THE CROW'S NEST

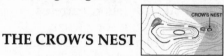

On the Crow's Nest, the Marines crawled from side to side to meet the direction of the current threat. PFC Nichols soon discovered that the NVA continually attempted to sneak up on the Marines by attempting to crawl surreptitiously up the steep, northern side of their position. PFC Nichols listened intently and, when he heard the NVA soldiers occasionally talking as they organized themselves for another attack on the Marines, he would disrupt their plans by rolling an M-26 fragmentation grenade into their midst.

PFC Mike Nichols: We crawled from just to the left of where we were facing. We crawled some from the right to the left, plumb over to the right side. The right side, which would have been to the company's left [Route 9]

side, was straight over there. It was real steep on that
side. But now that was the side they were throwing
most of the ChiComs from. They crawled up that side. I
don't remember how many M-26s we had up there, but
I remember just every now and then, you know, we'd
get to hearing them talk and we'd chuck one over there.
And, you know, you'd hear them scream and holler and
go on whenever those M-26s would go off.

For the past two hours the battle raging at the Crow's Nest
had been fought at a distance of less then 15 yards, easy throwing distance for a ChiCom grenade, even uphill. Sometimes,
though, the NVA soldiers managed to get even closer in the
darkness and the confusion. Corporal Howell found himself in
one of those situations when the two opposing forces suddenly,
and unexpectedly, confronted one another.

Corporal Kevin "Canadian" Howell: It was pitch black;
we were lying down, and all of a sudden, there were
feet all around us. We knew they were coming up but
we didn't know they were that close. They had slithered
somewhat. And then they jumped up and started running and we just jumped up and started fighting. They
surprised us and we surprised them; we just went at it,
kind of like a bar fight. I had that CAR [short-barreled
M-16] to start with and that went sailing somewhere
and we just started going at it. I had a Kabar. Used that.
Just kept at it, hacking and slashing. And they just fell
down. It wasn't anything like you see in the movies. A
guy gets hurt; gets a Kabar up against the side of his
head or across their neck or whatever, just falls down.
You could smell their breath when you went at it. And
they were easy to throw. They were easier to, like, knock
a weapon away from them or knock a bayonet away
from them. Even with a Kabar, you could outfight them.
But they swarmed you, three or four at a time. There
was a lot of them was what it was.
My jaw was broken on the right side, which I didn't
know about. I just knew there was a lot of pain. And I
was bayoneted in both hands, in the right arm and in
the face.
Corporal Howell witnessed an amazing sight, one which

left even the Marines in disbelief. Corporal Howell saw their supposedly fallen comrade, PFC Arthur, rise to his feet and kill an NVA soldier with his Kabar fighting knife.

Corporal Kevin "Canadian" Howell: Arthur was knocked down and out and we thought he was dead. We actually moved his body over from behind my position over to the right. When they swarmed up from the right, as they come up the gully, there was a lot of fighting going on. I turned around to come back. He was

fighting with an NVA soldier and he stabbed him to death and he fell down and died. He got to his feet after we thought he was dead. I saw it with my own eyes that he got up and grabbed an NVA soldier by the throat and stabbed him in the chest and killed him and fell down dead with him. It was a Kabar. Then we moved his body over more to the left of my position, behind me, because the enemy seemed to be coming up the gully from the right, more than from the left. And we didn't want

High School graduation photo of PFC Lawrence Arthur. (Credit: Virtual Wall)

to step on him. It wasn't that big a position.

He was the first casualty and he was lying there. But, let's face it, we were fucking busy. There was no corpsman. Couldn't call a corpsman. Couldn't take care of him. Couldn't do anything. We figured he was dead. He was probably stunned by the blast as well as being hit by shrapnel. When he came to during the attack, they were boiling up over that right gully, up into our position. He was a true Marine, all the way from start to finish.

Although the NVA had been forced to withdraw a short distance backward, they continued to throw grenades at the Marines in the Crow's Nest. A few moments later, one such grenade exploded so close to Corporal Howell that it set his trousers on fire, probably caused by the still-burning gunpowder and portions of the fuse.

Corporal Kevin "Canadian'"Howell: Something went
'boom!' and my uniform trousers caught on fire.

Corporal Howell quickly patted out the flames, then continued the fight. PFC Croft later jokingly told him, "Canadian,
you were okay in the fight until your pants caught fire, but
then you weren't worth a shit."

Although they themselves were locked in deadly combat,
the Marines on the Crow's Nest continued to look down at the
rest of the Foxtrot Marines on the ridge below who, in their
estimation, were suffering even worse.

PFC Harold Blunk: All during this action up at the
Crow's Nest, the guys down at the Ridge were getting
pulverized. It never stopped down there.

THE SOUTHERN SLOPE (away from Route 9)

In the occasional bright burst of light created by a
descending flare, the Marines along the southern slope could
see NVA troops at the base of the ridge, regrouping to form yet
another assault.

Lance Corporal Robert Kincaid: We could see them.
When illumination went up, I could make out individual targets. With that shotgun I couldn't reach them
once it got to where I was comfortable to expose myself
once I'd built up a little intestinal fortitude. I had targets but I couldn't hit them at 100 meters. Kohler stayed
pretty busy with the M-60. He had a lot of targets. I just
snapped ammo belts for him. I remember that the gun
got hot and we had 'cook-offs.' We didn't have a barrel
to change. We were having some 'cook-offs' and had to
cool down. But he didn't have a rifle and I just had that
shotgun so we just stayed in there for a God-awful long
time.

At one point they ran out of ammunition, but the ubiqui-
tous Lance Corporal Cutbirth was there to provide more.

Lance Corporal Robert Kincaid: Kohler and I ran out of ammo for the machine gun. I can remember that he was calling for ammunition and it began to appear. One of the other platoons—it wasn't 3rd Platoon—had M-60 ammo and they brought it over to us. Kohler continued firing and I continued to feed ammo for him. I remember we threw all the grenades we had. We didn't have anything else. We didn't have any claymores or anything. I remember that we threw every grenade that we had. I had a grenade pouch on my leg.

The Marines continued to be hit by a constant stream of RPGs. Lance Corparal Mylin had cause to be thankful for their earlier preparations when they had dragged a fallen log up the hill and placed it in front of their hole.

Lance Corporal Steve Mylin: That night when we got attacked, that log flew up in the air. It may have got hit by a rocket. I can remember them hitting that log that we put in front of our hole. I can remember that log flipping. It really jarred it and some shrapnel came in the hole and got me in the hand. I didn't even know it. All I could remember was, it was like a concussion and gunpowder smell.

THE EASTERN END (facing the Crow's Nest)

Adding a surreal effect to the battle was the sound made by the illumination rounds as they descended, an almost-comic *whoop-whoop-whoop* sound.

PFC Kevin Henry: I remember that weird sound that those night illumination parachutes used to make.

PFC Mark Woodruff: Kevin and I used to joke about them sounding like the noises one of the Three Stooges used to make in those old movies. You know: *whoop, whoop, whoop, whoop, whoop.*

Sergeant Joseph Quinn: I remember I was throwing rocks out there. I threw, like two or three rocks out and then I threw a grenade. We didn't have a whole lot of ammo and I guess we were watching our rounds.

Directly behind Sergeant Quinn and PFC Woodruff, 2nd Platoon's corpsman established a makeshift aid station. As Marines were wounded, they would either drag themselves over to this location or be assisted by their friends. The corpsman and his patients were only about 20 yards behind the perimeter defenses and simply lay on the ground.

Sergeant Joseph Quinn: Right behind us was the medic. That's where they were taking the wounded. They were pretty well fully exposed.

THE COMMAND POST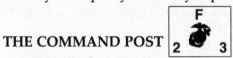

Gunnery Sergeant Ralph Larsen: When the flares started coming in, that helped us a lot. That put them more on the defensive and more hesitant to be standing up and heading into the fray. That helped a lot. And then when they brought Puff in and those long burst from miniguns just peppering the ground, that of course helped us a lot. The flares and that and the artillery is what saved us. Our supporting arms saved us. Without that it would have been, 'Hey, What happened to Custer?'

I am fortunate in this. I ain't saying that I'm not concerned about my safety but this never bothered me. I was always able to do my job, whatever it was. And that I'm thankful for. I didn't feel any fear then as I hadn't before. You know, you're shooting and they're shooting and somebody isn't going to make it. And that's the way it goes.

LZ HAWK

In the early morning hours two Marines managed to make it back to LZ Hawk from Foxtrot's battle up on the ridge. These were Marines who had been cut off from the main perimeter and decided to make their way on their own. The Battalion

Commander became concerned that there might be other Foxtrot Marines out there, cut of from their unit and needing help. Colonel Davis wanted the two tanks, parked along LZ Hawk as part of its perimeter defense, to proceed up Route 9 and look for any possible stragglers.

2nd Lieutenant William Tehan: And then, this is about 4:00, 5:00 in the morning, there were a couple of guys on the LP or something that made it into LZ Hawk. We thought they were missing. Anyway, they made it into LZ Hawk. There was two of them at first. And when that happened, Davis was concerned that there were other Marines who had been pushed off the position and were somewhere between Foxtrot Ridge and LZ Hawk. So there were two tanks in the position, one of them was right off of Route 9 and the other one was down about a hundred yards, pointed toward the west down along Route 9. In other words they were there to take advantage of the field of fire they had there where Route 9 was, headed toward the west, toward Khe Sanh. There were places made for them there in the lines at LZ Hawk. Davis was concerned there were other Marines who were trying to make it back into our position that couldn't make it back to Foxtrot. Davis then argued with somebody on the phone. I don't know if it was the Tank Company Commander or the Platoon Commander, but he argued with somebody on the phone. He told them what he was going to do and they didn't want to do it. He just said, 'They're my tanks and I'm going to do it.'

When Colonel Davis spoke directly to the sergeant in charge of the two tanks there at LZ Hawk, the sergeant too wanted nothing to do with what he saw as a totally ill-conceived plan. Tanks never operate without infantry support, especially at night. They are far too vulnerable to close-in attack, and the NVA were well-supplied with RPGs, easily capable of knocking out a tank and killing its crew with one hit. The tankers also knew the terrain in that area: full of scrub and brush and elephant grass that provided ideal cover for any NVA troops lying in ambush. To add to all this, the ground to the north of Route 9 rose up sharply in many places, meaning

that the NVA would be able to fire down on the tanks where
their armor was thinnest. But Colonel Davis wasn't to be dis-
suaded and so promised them a platoon of infantry to escort
them.

2nd Lieutenant William Tehan: So Davis got the [tank]
Platoon Sergeant and told him he was going to go
down and try to sweep the road and pick up any
Marines that were trying to make it into the position.
The Platoon Sergeant wanted nothing to do with it. He
wasn't being a coward or anything. He just realized that
he didn't want to take two tanks down the road in the
middle of the night; it was still dark. And so Davis said,
'Well, I'll give you infantry.' Well, we didn't have any
infantry at LZ Hawk. We had Bravo 1/12 and we had
the 81s and we had these two tanks.
   I was extra and so they said, 'Okay, what we'll do is
Lieutenant Tehan will take a platoon from 81s.' A platoon from 81s ended up being, like eight, maybe ten
people. We had two M-60 machine guns from 81s. We
all took ammo. The plan was, we were going to go
down the road and pick up any Marines that were out
there trying to get back to Hawk.

Lieutenant Tehan set out in pitch-black darkness, leading
his little convoy. The noisy, smelly diesel tanks clanked and rat-
tled and made their presence easily known to anyone within
hundreds of yards. The Marines all knew that, just over a mile
away, hundreds of NVA—many of them armed with RPGs—
swarmed around Foxtrot Company. They also knew that it was
very likely that, as part of their attack plan on Foxtrot
Company, the NVA would have ambushes in place along
Route 9 to thwart any possible rescuers from Khe Sanh or LZ
Hawk.

2nd Lieutenant William Tehan: So, somewhere around
4:00, 4:30, 5:00, it was maybe an hour before daylight,
we took off very slowly. So we took off and the two
tanks were maybe 50 yards apart, and a two-man
machine gun team, two riflemen and myself were sort
of walking about 25 yards up ahead of the lead tank.
And then the other four or five Marines with the other

A Marine M-48 tank operates along Route 9.
(Credit: Paul Marquis)

machine gun were walking behind the following tank.
So it was sort of a ragtag-type thing. We walked down
maybe 100 or 150 yards and then we heard something.
It wasn't anything but we stopped for a second. And
then we moved out again. We weren't moving very fast.

15 | DAWN APPROACHES AS THE MARINES WAIT EXPECTANTLY

The battle continued both on the ridge and the Crow's Nest. The Marines of Foxtrot were only too aware that dawn was approaching. Everything in their training and experience told them that, if they can only hold on until daylight, they might survive. Daylight would bring helicopter gunships and fixed-wing air support. Until then, the Marines of Foxtrot knew that they were on their own.

PFC Kevin Henry: I figured if we could live to see the sun come up we'd be alright, because we knew the air would be coming in.

THE CROW'S NEST

There were no more grenades on the Crow's Nest. Beside throwing rocks, the Marines even began shooting harmless signal flares in the general direction of the enemy. One of the Marines had several "pop-up flares" generally used to signal the return of an ambush patrol or an LP. The flares were aluminum and cylindrical in shape, about the size of a flashlight.

PFC Harold Blunk: There were bodies in front of us, but they were being pulled back. They were disappearing. They were pulling back wounded at this point. And there was a lull. At this point we had no more grenades. One of these guys had those aluminum flares

and he picked one up and I picked one up and we fired
them, *phhhew*, into the elephant grass. You could hear
the NVA in the elephant grass down the hill there, and
we'd fire at them because we knew they were still there.

The Marines strained their eyes into the darkness in front
of them, always alert for the little flash of light that indicated
another ChiCom being readied. The Marines were thus given
perhaps half a second in which to kill the NVA soldier before
he had time to throw it.

PFC Robert "Hillbilly" Croft: When they pulled the
cord on those ChiComs, I don't know if they realized it
or not, we just kept aimed in toward that place. When
we saw one of those little flashes, when they pulled the
striker on that ChiCom, we let them have it then
toward that direction. They were trying to come up.
They were coming up from the other side. They were
desperately trying to take us so they could be on top of
the company. They were coming up from the opposite
side of where the company was.

For most Marines, the worst job of all in the rear areas and
base camps was emptying and then burning the collected
refuse from the "outhouse" toilets. It was a necessary job for
health and sanitation reasons, but everyone deplored the fly-
blown, maggot-ridden job and its incredible stench. Now a
new leaf had been added to these Marines' *What's the Worst Job
in the World?* book.

PFC Robert "Hillbilly" Croft: When it settled down a
little bit, there was a little whispering between each
other, you know. And one of the guys on the Crow's
Nest turned to me and said, ' Man I sure would like to
be in the rear burning them shitters right now.'

Out of grenades and almost out of ammunition, some of
the Marines ventured out into the darkness and down the
slope slightly to gather weapons and ammunition from the
dead NVA soldiers lying there.

Corporal Kevin "Canadian" Howell: We ran down and

grabbed some rifles and brought them back up. I brought three rifles back up. And we took some ammo off their cartridge belts. I'm pretty sure Mouse went down with us. He looked like a PF [South Vietnamese 'Popular Forces' soldier]. Itty bitty little guy. Kept his hair cut just like a PF and he was very, very quiet. But he was a great practical joker. He was Hillbilly's a-gunner.

THE WESTERN FINGER

At the western finger the new defensive line continued to hold. Most of the handful of Marines who formed this line didn't have holes and simply lay flat on the ground. Lieutenant Dito continued to move back and forth checking the Marines in this area.

2nd Lieutenant Ray Dito: That's pretty much the way it went. I kept making that triangle. I remember talking to Holt, each time letting him know what I was doing. I'd say, 'I'm going back up to the CP' or 'I'm going over to the other side of the perimeter. Hold what you got.' And then I'd ask, 'How's your ammunition? What's your status?'

LZ HAWK

Lieutenant Tehan's scratch convoy of two tanks and a handful of Marines on foot continued to proceed westward along Route 9, hoping to find any stragglers or survivors who had made it to the road. Eventually they got to a point on the road where Foxtrot Ridge, as it was already dubbed, lay directly to their left. Still there was no sign of stragglers or survivors.

2nd Lieutenant William Tehan: So we got down probably 500, 600, yards to the turnoff, the one to the right that lead up to the Khe Sanh Combat Base. We could see the firefight; we could see the small arms fire. So we were maybe one-third the way down the Foxtrot Ridge position. I called back and asked, 'What do you want us do? We haven't found anybody.' Then there was a little

bit of discussion about whether we were going to take
the tanks into Khe Sanh, just keep on going west, or
going to turn around. I was talking to Colonel Davis on
the radio, and the Tank Platoon Sergeant was there but
he wasn't participating.

Rather than waste their trip, it was decided that the tanks
should use their powerful 90-mm main guns in support of the
beleaguered Foxtrot Company. Lieutenant Tehan tried unsuc-
cessfully to contact Lieutenant Jim Jones, but was able to speak
to Colonel Davis who could relay the message.

2nd Lieutenant William Tehan: They asked how many
rounds the tanks had. Between the two of them, they
had maybe 15 or 20 beehive [antipersonnel] and maybe
another 25 HE [high explosive]. It was around 50
rounds of something you could shoot at a hill. It was
decided that we would shoot at the base of the hill.
Now, I tried to raise Jim in Foxtrot. I had only one
PRC25 radio. There were the radios in the tanks, but I
didn't go back because the tanks were loud and noisy. I
switched freqs [radio frequencies] and tried to talk to
Jim but I couldn't raise Jim for some reason. And then I
went back to Davis and I told him I couldn't make contact. Davis was talking to Jim, but Jim and I couldn't
talk to each other, even though he was only 800 yards
away from me. It was right around that deep valley and
up the other side. So it was decided that we would
shoot at the base of the hill where we wouldn't have
any chance of putting anything into our guys on the top
of the ridge.
When the Tank Platoon Sergeant got off the vehicle, he
and I talked. He didn't want to do it. I said, 'Look,
we're just going to start left to right and you're going to
shoot left to right. When we get all the way over to the
right, and I was pointing at that position in the darkness, we're just going to come back and then by that
time you shouldn't have any ammo and we're going to
get out of here.' So I put the one machine gun team
down right off of Route 9. I just put them in maybe 10
feet off the road, just where it started to slope down. I
put them down a little bit, one so that if the tank fired

over them, the tank wouldn't blow their heads off. Then the other team was facing to the south also, because we didn't think any of the NVA were on the north side of Route 9. It didn't seem like they were there. We hoped they weren't there.

Just as dawn was beginning to break, the two steel behemoths blasted away at the base of the ridge and at any NVA lurking there. They fired as quickly as they could reload, stitching a pattern from one end of the ridge to the other, and then back again.

2nd Lieutenant William Tehan: It was just starting to get light, so the tanks started shooting from left to right and then went right to left and they shot up their ammo. We sort of fired down at the base, though the tanks couldn't depress all the way to the base of the hill because, when you're on Route 9, that's a pretty steep little valley in there. But they fired maybe two-thirds the way down the hill.

As agreed, the tanks signaled when they had used up all their main gun ammunition and spun back around, heading back to LZ Hawk. In their haste to return, they immediately set a pace the Marines on foot couldn't match. Lieutenant Tehan sprinted after them to get them to slow.

2nd Lieutenant William Tehan: It was agreed the Tank Platoon Sergeant was going to start waving when he was finished and we'd get up and move. Well, we started moving and he started going about ten miles an hour. He just wanted to get the hell out of Dodge. I finally got a hold of him on his tank radio and we walked the two vehicles into LZ Hawk.

16 | DAYLIGHT BEGINS TO BREAK AND HOPES ARE RAISED

Dawn began to break on Foxtrot Ridge. It came slowly, changing the blackness of night first into a darkish gray. The relief on the Marines' faces, even in that half-light, was clearly visible. Despite all the blood and gore they had seen, and despite—or maybe because of—their absolute certainty that they would never see another sunrise, broad smiles broke out on many Marines' faces. Daybreak. The NVA would now withdraw as, within moments, the Marines could expect to see air support arrive. Their collective euphoria soon dissipated as the Marines realized that the battle continued. The NVA had not withdrawn. They were still intent on killing the Marines of Foxtrot Company and seizing the ridge.

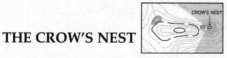

THE CROW'S NEST

Corporal Kevin "Canadian" Howell: The only thing I was waiting for was the sun to come up. We were kind of hoping like, okay, now that it's daylight, it's time for them to go away; it's the rule. You know, and they're breaking the rule. Even in boot camp, 'Hey, they'll hit you at night but then they're gone in the morning.' I'm saying, 'Damn, why are they still shooting?'

Like Corporal Howell, most of the Marines of Foxtrot assumed that the fighting would end at daylight. They had rationed their remaining supply of ammunition accordingly.

Now, as the battle continued, most of them had precious little, if any, ammunition left with which to defend themselves. PFC Gentry found himself precisely in this situation.

> **PFC Chris Gentry:** We were all out of ammunition. We had nothing left. This machine gunner had been blazing at us for hours. As it was daylight, Mike Nichols screamed at me, just literally screamed at me, 'Shoot!! Shoot!! Shoot!!' Well I didn't have any M-16 ammunition left. We saw this NVA soldier was low-crawling right up towards us, and so I just stood right up and aimed my M-16 at him. It was empty, and he turned around and scurried back.

As he "faced down" the NVA soldier with his empty weapon, PFC Gentry saw an even greater threat. Less than ten yards away, the RPD light machine gun, which had been tormenting them for hours, began blazing away in the direction of PFC Nichols. The RPD, a variant of the AK-47 assault rifle, fired the same caliber bullet but was equipped with bipods and a heavier barrel. Also, it was fed by a 100-round metal drum. The RPD machine gunners carried several of these drums and reloaded their weapons by removing the empty drum and replacing it with a loaded one.

> **PFC Chris Gentry:** Well, at the same time I saw this RPD machine gun in front of us and the guy was firing over towards Nichols' position. I dropped back down in the hole and I heard him drop the drum off and I knew he was changing the drum.

PFC Gentry knew he had only one chance to save PFC Nichols and probably himself, too. Still crouching in his foxhole and out of ammunition, he grabbed his entrenching tool and dashed toward the prone NVA machine gunner. With an almighty golf-like swing, he smashed the metal blade of the entrenching tool at the soldier's head.

> **PFC Chris Gentry:** I went out there with my entrenching tool and hit the gunner. I took the machine gun away and carried it back to the position with a couple of drums of ammunition. I hit him in the head as hard

as I could. There was no idea of heroic measures. This son of a bitch was going to chew away the extra inch of my foxhole and was going to kill me. And that's the only reason I got out of that foxhole.

As he gathered up the weapon and the ammunition, PFC Gentry also caught sight of the enemy's ammunition cache and the damage wrought by the Marines' defense.

PFC Chris Gentry: He was straight out in front of me, probably 20 feet. We were not quite to the crest of the hill in our position, so it was almost perfectly flat for about 30 or 40 feet on top of this hill. And then it sloped off very dramatically behind him. There was a big bomb crater back there and a number of dead NVA soldiers in this bomb crater and a lot—a lot!—of equipment in this bomb crater.

PFC Nichols was a grateful spectator to PFC Gentry's action, and to the NVA bullets kicking up dirt as they hit all around him.

PFC Mike Nichols: I remember realizing how crazy old Chris was. He was laughing and hollering when he hit the top of the hill with that machine gun, that gook machine gun. I mean they were burning us up, but they were firing over, up because we were laying on that kind of flat plateau there. But they were burning around his feet up that hill. One thing that sticks out in my mind was when Gentry come back on top of that hill with that machine gun, that gook machine gun, a-laughing and a-hollering and the dirt was beating up all around him.

It was quickly decided to place the newly acquired machine gun so that it could cover the "saddle" area and also could bring fire to bear on NVA soldiers still down on the finger area of the ridge below and now visible in the daylight. But the Marines on the ridge below had ears finely tuned to the distinctive sound of the NVA weaponry and, just as they had done for the past six hours, returned fire as if by reflex.

PFC Chris Gentry: We put the machine gun on what would have been our six o'clock position because part of the company at daylight had still been overrun. We were telling them to shoot and—I can't remember who—fired off about 50 rounds of machine gun ammunition, and you know an AK is an AK is an AK. Then all of a sudden the people from the company perimeter started shooting up at us. I guess they thought we'd been over-run and here's this distinctive North Vietnamese machine gun firing down towards the company. So after taking a couple of incoming friendly rounds from the company, we stopped using the machine gun over there.

Despite their disappointment over the NVA's not with-drawing, it soon became clear that daylight would bring even greater suffering to the NVA. Danger still lurked everywhere, but the Marines were increasingly confident. Although out-numbering them by a ratio of 10:1, the NVA were unsuccessful in seizing the Crow's Nest even after continuing and relentless attempts.

PFC Robert "Hillbilly" Croft: I think we had them pret-ty well 'whooped.' They just didn't send enough. They just thought they'd overrun us, you know.

THE WESTERN FINGER

For most of the Marines of Foxtrot, daylight provided the first opportunity to assess the situation and get some bigger view of the battle. It also provided them a welcome opportuni-ty to put their marksmanship skills to good use.

PFC Dave Kinsella: There was a gook down in the bomb crater at the very end of the finger. It was on the north side, the bomb crater there. He had a machine gun and he kept firing up at us. He'd pop up out of that hole and you could see him, and he'd fire a few rounds and then he'd duck down. Everybody was trying to get him every time he came up. I shot at him a number of times, and I think somebody finally got him because he never came back up.

With the sun now visible on the horizon, a Piper Cub spotter plane arrived overhead. The little two-seater, propeller-driven plan circled lazily overhead, looking for NVA troop concentrations and preparing air strikes against them. As the pilot circled, he observed: 'NVA bodies litter the area around Foxtrot's position.' He also observed that hundreds of NVA troops remained in the area and that it was therefore not yet safe for helicopters to approach. There would be no medevacs or resupply for the Marines of Foxtrot until the NVA withdrew or were killed.

2nd Lieutenant Ray Dito: That's about it until the dawn broke and then we got the aircraft above, and we had a better picture of what was going on, what the situation was, and how desperate things were. But then that also spelled the difference because they were able to bring in support. I remember Jones saying that, 'We have air on station,' and that they were now going to start hammering them and trying to relieve us. I distinctly remember seeing Dickie Cutbirth. He almost looked like he was enjoying himself. Maybe he was just happy at that point that the sun was up and he was still alive and kicking at that point. Things looked like they were turning in our favor.

THE SOUTHERN SLOPE (away from Route 9)

In the daylight, Sergeant Pressler could now see both the southern and the northern sections of the perimeter from his raised position with the mortar tube. Looking southward at one point in the battle, he saw a fascinating spectacle of courage and the will to survive.

Sergeant Hubert "Dick" Pressler: There was one guy, and I don't know who the gentleman is, but he jumped out of the foxhole, stabbed an NVA soldier in the neck who was close to the perimeter, and then jumped back in and continued fighting. I saw it. I saw the guy do it. It amazed me. Basically there was two or three in the foxhole, and they were firing. Then all of a sudden this one guy went down to reload and the NVA was coming right towards them. All of a sudden it was like, 'Well, you ain't gonna get me!' He jumped right out of the hole and went screaming—he didn't have to go far. Then in hand-to-hand combat, he got the guy with a knife, in his throat or the upper part of the neck. He got him a couple of times and then turned around and got right back in the foxhole.

Sergeant Pressler, too, heard the distinctive sound of PFC Gentry's RPD machine gun firing from the Crow's Nest.

Sergeant Hubert "Dick" Pressler: Then there was the Crow's Nest. The thing that really amazed me, while we were doing the battle, all of a sudden they started firing. You know and I know the difference between an AK sound and everything else. They started firing and the first thing that goes through everybody's mind is, 'They got the Crow's Nest.' Well, they didn't have the Crow's Nest. The people that were up there in the Crow's Nest ran out of ammo so they crawled out and brought their guns and ammo back into their perimeter and used that to fire over our heads to protect us from anything coming in.

THE EASTERN END (facing the Crow's Nest)

The battle had raged hard and long for men who were tired even before it began. Events would occur that caused those present to never again expect "absolute" answers or full understanding of anything. Many of the Marines would walk away with conflicting memories and large "blind spots" in their recollections. Once such incident occurred with PFC Woodruff in the early morning hours.

PFC Mark Woodruff: Just after daybreak, I was sharing my foxhole with the corpsman. I can't remember his name, but he was that big red-headed guy. Good guy, very 'gung ho.' I guess Quinn had to go check the lines or something and so the corpsman sort of grabbed an available spot. Anyway, by now we've got enough light to see and we're looking to our front and this guy says,

'Look out!' I can see he's pulling the pin and about to throw a grenade. Well he does and I watch him heave it out there and then I guess I'm counting off in my mind, 'One. Two. Three...' I crouch down waiting for it to explode. And of course, it goes *Boooom*!! and I'm thinking, 'What the hell is this guy doing?' But I look at him and he's got this big smile on his face, and he says, 'Did you see that? It hit that gook in the chest and dropped right between his legs before it went off!' I knew then that one of us was starting to flip out. Either he was seeing gooks where they weren't or I wasn't seeing them where they were. I looked at his face and I thought, 'One of us is going crazy,' but I didn't know which one.

LZ HAWK

Safely back at LZ Hawk with his little convoy, Lieutenant Tehan reflected on their activities. As he did so, he empathized more and more with the tankers and their reluctance to go on that mission. Increasingly, he came to believe they were probably right all along.

2nd Lieutenant William Tehan: If you were going to sit down and say, 'How do you do a rescue mission?' the way we did it was not the way to do it. It was just sort of an agreement that we were '. . . going to go sort of down here and sort of do this and, if this happens, we were sort of going to do this and . . .' Thank God, you know—and this is me guessing, I have nothing to base this on—if the NVA heard the tanks coming down the road, which they probably wouldn't have paid attention to with all the artillery coming in, by the time they realized we were on the road behind them and were shooting them up, it's probably a very good thing we didn't stay around where we were. Nobody shot at us. They were probably figuring, 'Where the hell is this coming from?' So, looking back at it, Colonel Davis shouldn't have put the two tanks out with so few people. We were not an infantry screen for those vehicles. We were minnows swimming in a pool of sharks, and I think we all knew it.

Regardless, the Marines of Foxtrot were forever thankful for the 50 rounds of high explosive and "beehive" rounds that no doubt killed many NVA soldiers hell-bent on killing Marines. Otherwise they might have done so.

17 | DAYLIGHT, BUT THE BATTLE CONTINUES

It was now about 7:30 AM. The sun shone bright and clear in announcement of yet another hot day. Daylight brought with it a renewed sense of confidence to the Marines of Foxtrot. Long hours of training, reinforced by actual combat experience in the past weeks and months, had instilled in the Marines a faith in their weapons and of their own skills. If they could see their enemy, the Marines of Foxtrot felt comfortable they could kill them. And now they could see them.

THE CROW'S NEST

Up on the Crow's Nest, the Marines were well aware of NVA soldiers on a ridgeline to their south. This was almost certainly one of the locations from which they had lobbed RPGs, angled high for maximum distance, throughout the previous night. The Marines would soon teach them something about the 7.62-mm M-14 and marksmanship.

> **PFC Robert "Hillbilly" Croft:** There was a ridgeline. If you'd went down again and came back on the other side, there was another ridgeline over there. And they were dug in it because we saw two gooks sitting over there. Well an M-16 wouldn't touch them. And the M-79 wouldn't go that far. And they were laughing. The two of them were sitting in a hole, and they were laughing because we couldn't hit them.

PFC Harold Blunk: At one point I was looking through my binoculars and we were looking over at that other ridge to the south, looking through the grass. All of a sudden, I turned to my right and the other fellow in my hole turned to his left and a round passed right between us. It just cracked in my ear and cracked in his ear. I then looked back in that same area with my binoculars and I saw two NVA with helmets on looking at us. It was far enough away, and there was a tree there in the grass next to them. That's when the M-14 really came into play. I said, 'Here, take the binoculars and look through there. I could see the tree and I cranked up the sights and looked on the map to see how far away it was and started firing with the M-14. The guy with the binoculars confirmed the kill. He confirmed that I took out the NVA. That was way over on the other side there. Might have been 600 meters.

But the NVA were still also in close contact with Foxtrot. PFC Blunk spotted what he thought was an abandoned RPD machine gun lying next to a dead NVA soldier in the grass to their front. He leaped to the opportunity to seize the weapon and use it in the Crow's Nest's defense.

PFC Harold Blunk: We were shooting way over there, but there was still things happening right in front of us. When we had some light to see by, I could see the bipods of this Chinese machine gun—maybe 25 or 30 feet in front of me—and what appeared to be a body behind it. And so I got up to go and get the machine gun and as I went to get it, this guy wasn't dead. I fired at him and the round went right between his legs and then my M-16 jammed. I literally ran back up the ridge, and this gook took off and ran in the opposite direction back down the ridge.

The Marines up on the Crow's Nest had the ideal vantage point from which to fire down onto the NVA soldiers continuing their attacks on the company below. Their bullets cracked loudly over the heads of the Marines. Because of the angle of their fire, their bullets passed only a few feet over the heads of the men forming the new defense line.

Robert "Hillbilly" Croft: Everybody had cramps from being in the hole, because the hole was so small. We didn't have all that much communication. Blunk did a good job on calling in the artillery and everything. But we were shooting over the company and everything. Well this could present a problem here, you know. Then finally everybody caught on, I reckon. I could see them come up from the other side. One gook, I bet we shot him I don't know how many times. They were coming up from the far end and over from the left a little bit.

THE WESTERN FINGER

With bullets occasionally cracking over their heads from the Crow's Nest, Lance Corporal Kinkaid now joined the new defense line facing the finger. To his front was the LZ; the brightly colored nylon mail bag still sat there. In it were several dozens of letters the Marines had written in the past few days.

Lance Corporal Robert Kincaid: The sergeant told us to bring that machine gun up and put in on the trail facing those mailbags, when we could identify each other, when we could tell we weren't shooting our own people. I would say, as a hunter, when you've got 'scope light.' So we brought the machine gun up and set it on the trail and collected some more ammunition. I ended up facing that way on the trail with Kohler and the machine gun. That's where I ended up. They had us shift over. And Charlie and I set the gun up on that trail down toward the mail bags.

THE EASTERN END (facing the Crow's Nest)

Someone, probably Sergeant Quinn, began laughing and yelling at the NVA soldiers undoubtedly still within earshot. It was a taunt, letting the NVA know that they had been beaten by the Marines who still remained, defiant. All around that side of the perimeter, the Marines joined in, yelling and laughing and swearing at the NVA. In what was probably abominable Vietnamese, the Marines strung together sentences filled with profanities clearly understandable to the NVA still present.

Sergeant Joseph Quinn: We were yelling, *Ho Chi Minh cac dau*, or something like that. But then they started responding to that. I remembered hearing the round come in. So, everybody got back in the holes.

An RPG round came hurtling in with its familiar *whooshing* sound as it flew through the air and then, a split second later, impacted with the loud *crunch* of its explosion. The momentary smell of gunpowder again filled the air. The round hit only a few feet behind Lance Corporal Cutbirth. Nearby, PFC Henry dashed to the aid of his friend.

PFC Kevin Henry: An RPG came in and slammed into the ground just in front of our hootch. This was just as it was becoming light. I have no idea what time it was. It was light and I saw Dickie lying there. I took senior lifesaving when I was at the University of Colorado, and I remembered how to do mouth-to-mouth resuscitation. I looked around at his body to see where he was hit, but I didn't see anything. But when I picked the back of his head up with my left hand, there was blood all over my hand. One of the things in mouth-to-mouth resuscitation is you want to clear the airway and you want to lay the neck back so that you have a clear air passage. You want to make a very, very tight seal and blow very, very hard. I remember doing this a countless number of times. I saw his chest rise and I saw his chest come down again and I thought that maybe there was, you know, something there.

18 | WAITING FOR HELP TO ARRIVE

By midmorning, the firing had diminished somewhat but the NVA were still clearly present and in large numbers. Helicopter gunships appeared occasionally and fired machine guns and rockets at NVA troops in the near distance. But the NVA were well-supplied with antiaircraft weapons, wheeled Chinese-made .51 caliber machine guns, that prevented any hope of helicopter landings. The wounded Marines still lay on the ground, being tended to as best they could by Foxtrot's corpsmen. Some of the wounded had continued to suffer and bleed since sustaining wounds in the opening moments of the battle, some seven or more hours ago.

Foxtrot would have to be relieved and reinforced the old-fashioned way by a ground attack by another rifle company, breaking through the encircling NVA. Word was soon passed to the Marines of Foxtrot that their brothers in Echo 2/3 were on their way.

THE COMMAND POST

Echo Company, about 120 strong and supported by the two tanks from LZ Hawk, was approaching via Route 9. Their presence was signaled when their Commanding Officer, Captain William Russell, ordered the tanks to fire on NVA troops they could see on the western finger of Foxtrot Ridge. But the distance and the angle precluded a good shot.

1st Lieutenant James Jones: When Echo Company came up to rejoin us, they were also on Route 9 and they had a couple of tanks with them. We knew we still had some bad guys in the perimeter in 1st Platoon's old area. Bill Russell tried to engage them with a tank round, but the line of fire was such that, by engaging them, if they would have missed, they would have engaged us. They actually did fire a couple of rounds but they skipped and it was too close. I asked them to end that mission. Then they started the overland march to come up on the hill.

THE CROW'S NEST

Everyone realized that it would take quite some time for Echo Company to arrive and there was no guarantee that they would actually make it. A large number of NVA troops were still in the vicinity, and it was quite possible that Echo would get bogged down in firefights and engagements along the way. So the Marines knew they would have to wait.

Because of the presence of aircraft in the vicinity, all artillery firing had been ceased for safety reasons. So PFC Blunk was "out of a job" as an artillery forward observer. PFC Blunk, however, was not the type of man who was comfortable just sitting around. For reasons that he doesn't even know, but ascribes as probably due largely to boredom, he decided he wanted to take a look further down the trail leading out of the Crow's Nest and heading east.

PFC Harold Blunk: I said, 'Who wants to volunteer?' I am a hyper kind of a guy. I can't sit still. That's all. There was no more fire missions now. It was daylight and we had fixed wing on station and so there was a 'check fire' on artillery. And one of the guys said, 'I'll go with you.' This guy and I went down the trail, going away from Foxtrot Ridge in the other direction. We came up on a bomb crater to the right of us on that trail. There were NVA in that bomb crater. They had RPG rounds and RPG launchers right on the edge of that bomb crater and all their gear and stuff right there. We were right on their flank, right on the side of them. We came right in there and took them out. I had a .45 and the other guy had the M-14. I didn't trust that M-16, and I figured where I was going at this point, a .45 would be appropriate. There were two NVA right there, looking up the hill. What was more terrifying than that —that seemed pretty easy—it was like slow motion. We came up and there they were, and I was on my belly and just squeezed off the rounds and I remember seeing daylight under the NVA guy. The .45 seemed to just pick him right up off the ground, and there was daylight underneath him from taking him out like that.

PFC Blunk took the dead NVA soldier's assault rifle. When one of the "dead" NVA soldiers moved, the other Marine shot him again with the M-14, providing a comic moment in the eyes of that Marine but also bringing a deadly fusillade down on them from NVA troops nearby.

Lance Corporal Doug "Deuce" Near at LZ Hawk, May 1968. (Credit: Author's Collection)

PFC Harold Blunk: Just at that moment when I was
there, this other Marine fired the M-14. He had it on automatic because there was some sort of muscle spasm or
something on one of the NVA bodies that I'd turned my
back on. And when he fired like that, the rounds came
out and my feet were like running but I wasn't moving
and he started laughing for a second. This automatic fire
plus my own .45 firing must have caught the attention of
the NVA occupying the next little ridgeline a few hundred
feet away. It wasn't visible from the Crow's Nest because
it was blocked by another one, but it looked directly
down on where we were now. And it was full of NVA.
The bomb crater was fully exposed to this; there was no
cover from that area. All I can remember is everything
moving around me, jumping up from being hit by bullets.
And this guy and I ran back up to the Crow's Nest and I
remember diving right in where Arthur was and I just
said, 'Holy shit! I don't know how we made it back.'

When he'd caught his breath, though, PFC Blunk realized he had
risked life and limb in his actions, but all he had to show for it
was one assault rifle. Meanwhile, back down that trail, there was
a whole armory of weapons and ammunition.

PFC Harold Blunk: And then I says to myself that here
I've got this AK-47 but there's more ammunition for the
RPD and of course there were all those magazines there.
So I said, 'Do you want to go back? Let's go back and get
the ammunition.' We went back, and this time I took the
.45 and an M-79 with a shotgun round in it. I don't know
what I was thinking of. I don't know what got into me. So
we went out there getting more ammunition and we
started scarfing up everything. As we're picking it all
up—they had all the stuff laid out there, staged, at the
edge of the bomb crater—the NVA saw us there and
opened up on us again. And then we just charged back to
the Crow's Nest.

PFC Blunk had gathered together a whole booty of supplies, including a dozen or more fully-loaded magazines for the
AK-47s and also several spare drums for their RPD light
machine gun.

PFC Harold Blunk: This time we'd got what we had and we weren't going out there any more. That was it. That was the end of that deal. Now we'd been resupplied. We had a lot of stuff. I went out there once and could have got killed. It didn't make sense: I came back with a friggin' rifle with one magazine! This isn't going to help our cause. Now, when I came back a second time, I've got a bag full of stuff. We had enough ammunition now that we could 'waste' it on targets that were farther away from us. Otherwise, we weren't firing until they were right on top of us. That's when I had a lot, maybe a dozen 30-round magazines. Now we're confident that we can fire this off.

THE EASTERN END (facing the Crow's Nest)

With Lance Corporal Cutbirth critically wounded and PFC Henry attempting to minister medical aid to him in the absence of the concussed corpsman, Lance Corporal Near took over the machine gun. He could see a long line of NVA troops, maybe 30 in number climbing a small hill a few hundred yards away. He immediately took them under fire, killing several and scattering the rest.

Lance Corporal Doug "Deuce" Near: I saw a line of gooks, kind of like they were in a hurry, and they were a ways out there and then, you know, I just opened up on 'em.

Although Lance Corporal Cutbirth didn't appear to have a pulse, PFC Henry continued giving what care he could. They were both fully exposed to the enemy fire which still cracked as bullets passed close by.

PFC Kevin Henry: I tried to bring him back and I thought that I had succeeded because his chest rose and fell several times. I kept thinking to myself, you know, this can't be real; this has to be a movie. Another distinct thought was that, 'My friends and family have absolutely no idea what's going on here right now.' But I felt no fear. I really didn't. But I just wanted to save him because he was such a good guy. I just tried to do everything I could because I liked him so much. He was such an affable, good-natured boy from Missouri. He had a good smile and he took to me and we got along very, very well, even though we were together for only a short period of time.

Despite all of PFC Henry's best efforts, it eventually became clear that Lance Corporal Cutbirth was dead, probably killed instantly by the head injury he sustained from the RPG shrapnel.

PFC Kevin Henry: The only reason his chest was rising and falling was because I was blowing into it. Every time I stopped, you know, nothing happened.

THE WESTERN FINGER

Lance Corporal Kincaid continued to guard that sector of the new defense line that looked straight onto the LZ and its mailbag. He observed two Marines, who had been in the thick of it all night, now proceeding on another dangerous mission. They were going to go down onto 1st Platoon's old area to ensure that the 60-mm mortar abandoned there along with a quantity of ammunition had, in fact, been rendered inoperable so that it could not be used against the Marines.

Lance Corporal Robert Kincaid: I remember then Chico Rodriquez from Chicago and Tex La Bonte. They were kind of like macho guys, 'You can't hurt me.' I remember they were bare chested. They didn't have a T-shirt on. Both of them had .45 pistols. They said that they had to go forward and I can't remember if they said they had to 'blow the tube,' or 'the tube had been blown and they had to make sure of it.' But it had something to do with the tube. So they crawled and went out that way. I heard pistol shots and, when they came back in, Rodriquez had an arm wound on his right upper arm almost into the shoulder. A slight penetrating wound, probably shrapnel or something like that. He was ignoring it, ignoring the pain; it would go away. They pulled back, went somewhere, I don't know. I was busy watching those mailbags.

LZ HAWK/Route 9

The Marines of Echo 2/3 had proceeded westward along Route 9 until they came abreast of the trail leading up to Foxtrot Ridge. After the tanks had fired a few rounds at the NVA, Echo Company began its movement off the road and onto the trail.

One of the Marines coming up with Echo Company was 22-year-old Sergeant Dale Dye. Sergeant Dye was a Marine Corps combat correspondent. His job was to document the activities of Marines in Vietnam and provide articles and news for service journals and newspapers. There were several units he frequently accompanied, one of them being Echo 2/3.

Sergeant Dale A. Dye. (Credit Dale Dye)

Sergeant Dale Dye: We were on Route 9. I heard that Fox had been in a hell of a fight off to our left. There was a massive kind of a high bunch of ground running up off to our south. You could see it from Route 9. There was kind of 'fingers,' like the fingers of a hand, and that's what it looked like to me. Some were higher than others and so on and so forth. I remember trying to figure out where they were, what was happening. You couldn't see the fight, at least from where I was you couldn't. We got orders, the word was just passed to me, that we were going to turn left and go off the road. So they formed us up in kind of a column and we started off toward those hills in a column. Immediately we came off the road, we went down into a little dip and then we started going up. And as we started going up we hit this damned elephant grass, this huge stuff, and I knew this was trouble.

It was painfully slow-going in the dense elephant grass. Because of the presence of NVA troops, Echo could not simply proceed up the trail in single file as Foxtrot had done. Instead, they were forced to deploy tactically. Knowing the urgency of their mission, the slow progress was particularly frustrating.

Sergeant Dale Dye: I was up around the company gunny, who had the radio operator with him. I was trying to follow it, and there was a real 'press' to get up there. And we were carrying extra stuff for them, extra ammunition, 60-mm mortar rounds. I was carrying a bunch of stuff, because I was 'lighter,' I guess, than the rest of the guys. I remember going uphill. We were kind of spread out and I was a little center-left of the line, I guess. And we were having real trouble staying tied in with each other. The gunny was pissing and moaning; you know there was a press to get up there. 'These guys are in trouble!' And about the time he said that, we got hit. We got hit forward on our right.

Echo Company was soon engaged in its own battle before their rescue mission had hardly begun.

Sergeant Dale Dye: When we got hit, everybody went down of course. It escalated into an immediate shit-fight on our right side. And we were trying to move the left flank over, to close on them from what would be their right flank. It was machine guns, and then when I started to move, we got rockets. They were RPGs: B40s. It really escalated and there was this sense of isolation. We knew that somewhere up above us was Foxtrot, but it was so dense with this elephant grass that you couldn't see anybody. It was the typical 'yelling at each other,' trying to figure out who was where and so on and so forth. I kept moving, sort of to my right front, trying to keep my eye on the gunny and the radio operator. I damned near walked into one of the bastards. The guy just scared the shit out of me. I saw him just ahead of me, and he was firing an SKS off to his left front. He didn't see me, I guess, and I killed him. And the gunny shit himself, thinking that I was firing into them. I finally walked up with him, actually it was kind of crawled up with him, and showed him this guy, and he said, 'Oh shit!' Because what that actually meant was we had gooks between us, sort of right center, and the left wing that he was trying to swing around. So he left then, and went behind me and over to the left and started trying to pull people up.

19 | A DESPERATE SITUATION, NO HELP REFUSED

It was nearly 12:00 noon, May 28. While Echo Company continued to fight its way toward Foxtrot Ridge, the Marines of Foxtrot were under continuing pressure by NVA troops, who no doubt hoped to deliver a coup de grace before help arrived. The aerial observer spotter plane drifting overhead had sighted a group of 30 NVA soldiers gathering on the southern slope of the ridge, forming up in anticipation of yet another attack. By now, Foxtrot's defenses were stretched so thin and their supply of ammunition was so low that such an attack might well prove successful. When an F-4 Phantom jet arrived "on station" and became available, it was decided to use it to attack these NVA troops, despite the dangerous proximity to Foxtrot's own Marines. This F-4 did not carry a load of bombs, but carried instead a payload of napalm. It was decided that the jet would drop its load of napalm on the NVA troops gathering at the base of the ridge on its southern slope.

The F-4 screamed in from the east at treetop level and roared past the ridge. This was only a "practice run" for the pilot, confirming the target, but it also assured the attention of every Marine on Foxtrot Ridge. Every eye was on the F-4 as it screamed past, made a great arcing loop and prepared for a second pass.

THE COMMAND POST

Lieutenant Jones was in radio contact with the pilot and, by this stage of the battle, was in no position to deny any help.

1st Lieutenant James Jones: The pilot seemed to have a good fix on us visually. It was a clear day. They were running the right direction. They made a practice pass before they went 'live.'

THE SOUTHERN SLOPE (away from Route 9)

Lance Corporal Mylin was located on the southern slope with the CP only a few yards behind him. He could hear a Marine in the CP directing the aircraft by radio. He could also hear the voice of the pilot, his tone somewhat garbled but still distinguishable, ring out through the radio's handset receiver.

Lance Corporal Steve Mylin: I can remember them saying, 'He's coming in low and it might be close.' There was somebody right behind me talking directly to the pilot. I'm not sure if it was an FO talking to him or our CO. From what I thought, it was our CO. I remember thinking, 'Man, that's cool that they can actually talk to the pilot.' And he said he was coming in close. He said, 'Be careful. Tell your men to get down because I'm coming in close.' And he did.

Lance Corporal Alan "Chief" Walker: It seemed like we could reach out and touch him, he was so close. When he turned, you could see inside his cockpit. Boy, he brought that F-4 down. He was low.

Lance Corporal Jim Chafin: I could look inside the air ducts of that jet. I could see the mask on the pilot's face. He was coming in that close and that low. I thought he was crashing. I didn't think he was getting up. Then he dropped that napalm and he shot straight up.

All eyes were on the F-4. So everyone also saw the two silver canisters, huge cylindrical containers of napalm, tumbling end over end as they fell to earth. As they tumbled closer, many Marines could make out the stenciled lettering along the canisters' sides. It was clear that they were going to hit extremely close, and every Marine ducked in anticipation.

THE EASTERN END (facing the Crow's Nest)

PFC Kevin Henry: That F-4 came by. He was low and close, right in front of our position. I remember seeing those napalm canisters come down, and I said, 'Oh man, we're in deep shit. Jones called them in close. Jones wasn't fooling around. There were boocoo gooks out there.

The napalm hit just 20 yards from the Marines' foxholes and an enormous wall of flame erupted skyward from one end of the ridge to the other along that southern slope. The heat was both instantaneous and unbearable. Primitive instincts immediately took over the actions of every man at Foxtrot Ridge. It took only a millisecond for each to respond, their survival depending upon getting away from that life-sucking heat. They withdrew from it as quickly as, only a few days ago, they might have responded when touching a lighted match.

Lance Corporal Steve Mylin: It was like right in front of us. It was like an explosion, like gasoline. You might have a second to jump after it caught on fire, to jump out of your hole and run.

Sergeant Joseph Quinn: If you'd stayed, you'd have been scorched. Just the heat chased you out of there.

Sergeant Dave McCoy: The first time they napalmed was on the south side. They were coming in really close, and when it hit, I mean everybody basically cooked a little bit on the face.

A wild, pell-mell scramble began, with the Marines crawling and stumbling backward over the crest of the ridge and partway down the northern slope, only stopping when the physical mass of the ridge itself shielded them from the intense heat still raging as the tall elephant grass added its fuel to the inferno.

Corporal Dave Smith: When the napalm came in, and that sheet of fire came up the south side, I grabbed my radio man and another Marine and pulled them over to the other side of the hill so we wouldn't get burned up.

Lance Corporal Curtis "Snake" Clark: It was the flames. They were coming toward us. And I ran toward the road [Route 9]. My pack caught on fire and my clothes were smoking, so I pulled those off. Just ripped those off and just dropped them. Clothes are smoking, running down the hill and ripping those off. Actually ran down the other slope trying to get away from it and then had to sort of crawl back up.

Sergeant Hubert "Dick" Pressler: I don't know how far we went. You could say halfway down the hill or a quarter of the way. I don't know. I was running like it was going out of style.

Sergeant Dave McCoy: I honestly thought it was coming in on us. I was ready for the barbecue sauce, I think. I was losing a lot of blood, but I crawled down over the side of the hill.

THE CROW'S NEST

The Crow's Nest was far enough away that it was untouched by the napalm. Because of the fire in the saddle area a few days ago, which had already burned off the grass and brush, the fire never spread in their direction. They were simply spectators to the whole event, but it was the worst possible spectacle they could have imagined.

PFC Mike Nichols: That was wild, too, when they dropped that napalm. We were sitting there looking at them. I remember seeing one guy on fire, running. I remember thinking, 'Shit, we're dead.' Because I remember seeing a bunch of guys running off the hill, off the Route 9 side. I remember seeing what looked like almost everybody, a-running off the mountain. And

I said, 'Oh shit!' Because the gooks were still in between us at that time. There was still a bunch of them in that saddle. That was probably the scaredest feeling that I had while I was there. I remember that the worst part about the whole deal, to me, was when they dropped the napalm. I thought, 'Oh hell. Katy bar the doors,' because they ain't even going to get that hill back. Hell, everything was on fire.

The Marines on the Crow's Nest now looked down at a ridge ablaze. The Marines, who had scrambled away from the flames, did so immediately and generally took only the weapons in their hands. What little spare ammunition they had, generally placed in or near their foxholes, now exploded and crackled in the fire that swept the ridge. While the napalm no doubt killed that group of NVA soldiers preparing to attack, the NVA seemed to have an endless supply of replacements.

PFC Harold Blunk: When the napalm hit and burned the company right off the ridge, I said, 'Throw some fire down there.' And when the guys on the ridge were running down the north side of the ridge, we threw some rounds down the south side to discourage any surviving NVA who might have thought of assaulting up the hill. The last thing I wanted was for the NVA to come up the south side of the ridge at the same time the company was coming back up the north side. And it could have happened because we were still in contact then. So we fired some rounds into the valley, hoping to hit somebody, but maybe even just fire over their heads, at least letting them know that there's somebody still up there firing down from the ridge.

THE NORTHERN SLOPE (facing Route 9)

Within moments, the entire company had scrambled over to the northern slope. The ground there was rock-strewn and barren. Its gradient was steep enough that the Marines apprehensively sheltering there stood precariously, ever at risk of tumbling unceremoniously down its incline. Their eyes darted to one another nervously, pausing momentarily when their eyes met. No words were spoken. They all knew how desperate their situation was.

Corporal Smith was armed only with a nine-pound rocket, intended for use in the 3.5-inch rocket launcher, which he found lying on the ground. It was about the size and shape of a bowling pin and he hefted it like a club, the only "weapon" he could find.

Corporal Dave Smith: When I pulled those two guys off the hill, I left my rifle and my radio because I had my hands full with those guys. So what I ended up picking up was a three-five round. And I had that in my hand and I said, 'My God!' At that point, I'm not a super religious guy, but I made peace with God and I said, 'I'm dying right now.' All of a sudden everything was so calm. I can still remember I had that three-five round in my hand and I was going to use that as a club because all I felt was going to happen was that, after that fire burned, here comes a human wave NVA attack over the hill.

Lance Corporal Alan "Chief" Walker: I do know that when that napalm hit and burned us off the ridge, my thoughts were that the gooks were going to be behind that fire. And as it burned us off, they would just assume our positions. I was thinking, 'How in the hell are we going to take back our positions?'

Lance Corporal Doug "Deuce" Near: I thought when we got to the top of the hill it was going to be 'Katy bar the door.' At that point, well, we had made it through here; it's daylight and now this happens to us. They drop it on our end of the ridge and chased us off the ridge. I had the M-14. I didn't have any more grenades. I didn't have much ammo left.

PFC Mark Woodruff: I had my .45 pistol and five rounds in the magazine. That's it. Nothing more. The situation couldn't get much worse.

No one was more aware of the need to reclaim the ridge than Lieutenant Jones. His more logical mind also considered an option that had not even occurred to the Marines of Foxtrot but might have led to disaster.

1st Lieutenant James Jones: As the fire burned itself out rather quickly, then my decision was easy: to try to get everybody to get back on top of that hill as opposed to pandemonium breaking out and turning into a ragtag outfit, racing toward Route 9.

Sergeant Hubert "Dick" Pressler: No sooner I got partway down the hill and then I look back and I hear somebody say, 'Attack!' Then the next thing you know we're going back up the hill. There was still fire there, but we were still going. And we were firing as we were going up the hill. But I know that it was still burning when I got back up there.

Lance Corporal Curtis "Snake" Clark: Some one—I mean it was just like out of a John Wayne movie—someone near me said, 'Let's take our hill!!' Or something like that and 'Charge!' And then we did a frontal assault back up the hill, across the top.

Sergeant McCoy continued to bleed badly and was too badly injured to make it back up the hill. He had suffered shrapnel wounds to the face earlier in the battle when he had been blown off the ridge and bullet wounds as he had scrambled back up. But he anticipated Lieutenant Jones' order and ensured his Marines would act as required.

Sergeant Dave McCoy: I told Chico, I said, 'Chico, as soon as the fire's gone, it's going to be a race to see who gets back up there first.' And I said, 'You've got to be there.' He said, 'I can't leave you.' And I said, 'Get your ass out of here.' He took off up there.

THE CROW'S NEST

The Marines on the Crow's Nest couldn't believe their eyes and the relief was palpable as they saw the Marines of Foxtrot come scrambling back up the northern slope of Foxtrot Ridge.

PFC Mike Nichols: Oh yeah! We were thrilled to death when we saw the company come back up.

While the Marines on the ridge below, sparingly using what little ammunition they had, advanced across the ridge, the Marines on the Crow's Nest rendered all help they could. PFC Croft, from his vantage on the Crow's Nest, could see NVA soldiers attacking up the southern slope as the Marines approached the opposite direction. He blazed away with the M-14 while others fired in support with captured NVA weapons.

PFC Robert "Hillbilly" Croft: We kept on because that napalm had burned all out on that side and the company was on the other side. They couldn't see them coming up so we figured we'd help out as much as we could.

FOXTROT RIDGE: The Main Perimeter

The Marines, crouching low, sprinted over the crest of the ridge and back toward their former positions. There was only sporadic gunfire. The Marines regained their defensive positions before the NVA could react in strength. In the near distance, just the other side of the blacked southern slope, NVA soldiers could be seen fleeing to the south. One of the attacking Marines was Lance Corporal Clark, now naked except for his boots, having shed his smoldering clothing moments before as he tumbled down the northern slope.

Lance Corporal Curtis "Snake" Clark: As we reached the top, I remember firing at soldiers running down the other side of the hill. The best way to describe it was like skeet shooting. I hit some and missed some. I was not concerned with ensuring who I shot at was hit. I wanted to shoot at as many as I could before they disappeared in the high grass.

As they looked around, the Marines of Foxtrot found their old positions were almost unrecognizable. Everything had been burned in the intense heat. Packs, clothing, cartridge belts, spare ammunition, everything that the Marines of Foxtrot possessed, was ash. The dead NVA soldiers, who lay scattered in front of each of their foxholes, were now charred. Hazy smoke still clung to the ground. It seemed like Foxtrot Ridge had been transformed into a scene straight out of hell.

Lance Corporal Doug "Deuce" Near: My poncho was virtually melted to the earth. I came back up and there it is. It's nothing but a puddle of plastic. I remember a live round going off underneath my foot when I was coming back up the ridge. I thought, 'Jesus Christ, I've been shot or something.' But it was a cookoff. I don't know what kind of round it was, but it went off underneath my foot. That does weird stuff to you, you know.

Corporal Dave Smith: And when I went back up, everything was burned up. Even my radio and my rifle burned up.

PFC Mark Woodruff: My pack and my cartridge belt had been laying right behind my hole. The cartridge belt, you know they were made out of that heavy canvas and they had all these little brass eyelets to attach gear to, well that had just disappeared. There was just this neat row of brass eyelets lying in a ribbon of ash. The fire had consumed everything but the metal.

When they had settled into their old positions, the Marines became aware of the devastating effect the napalm had on their NVA attackers. As they looked down the southern slope of Foxtrot Ridge, they could see the NVA assault wave that had prompted the napalm attack. Their bodies were now added to the hundreds of others who had died at the hands of Foxtrot Company and their supporting arms. The southern slope was now a sea of charred bodies.

Lance Corporal Robert Kincaid: This gook was burned alive. I remember that he was in a prone position, laying down dead. His hand had grasped a tree or a root or a rock or something and he had like strained himself up serpentine, kind of strained from the waist to raise his head up out of the dust. He had died in that position, and it was kind of like he was petrified there. Holding onto this tree stump or something like he was trying to pull himself up off the ground and was just like frozen, suspended in time.

Lance Corporal Steve Mylin: They were right down there where they dropped the napalm. That's the whole reason why they dropped the napalm. They said there were gooks sneaking back up the hill the next day. They were just like charred statues, leaning forward, in a crouching stance.

Sergeant McCoy, his face unrecognizable from the swelling and too weak to climb by himself, was assisted back onto the ridge by Lance Corporal Rodriguez.

Sergeant Dave McCoy: Then Chico hustled back over, and all this time I'm shooting at North Vietnamese down there. He brought another Marine with him, maybe Mylin, and they were shooting because I couldn't crawl back up. I didn't have any strength left. It was easy for me to slide down. He drug me back up to the middle of the hill and put me right in the middle of all them 60 mortars that were spread out all over the place. About the only thing he said to me was, 'Man, you wouldn't believe how your face has swollen up!'

LZ HAWK/Route 9

The Marines of Echo Company continued in their unremitting approach to assist Foxtrot.

Sergeant Dale Dye: That elephant grass holds the heat and we began to lose people, you know. You couldn't see the guy. As we moved and as we started going up, we started hearing fire. Now at that point it wasn't a full-pitched firefight. I'd heard a hundred of those. You'd hear an RPG every once in a while and then you'd hear a *cack-cack-cack . . . cack-cack-cack*.

First Platoon, Echo 2/3 at LZ Hawk immediately after the battle.
(Credit: Louis Lopez)

You know, it was kind of a sporadic contact thing.
We were kind of on line moving up into this thing.
At that point I remember the tanks started to fire. It
scared the beejeesus out of me! I didn't know what
the fuck it was. I figured it out after a while, but it
sent everybody to ground immediately. I think they
were firing right over our heads. And the deal was
the company gunny got a little worried about that
because these are high-velocity rounds. You know,
flat trajectory, high velocity. And they were cranging
'em. You could hear them go right over our head.
And I said, 'Hello!' I was hoping that somebody had
figured out, or told them, that we were up here,
moving in this direction. Obviously, they did. I
mean, the company commander must have been
talking to the tankers. They were hitting targets and
that's when we began to see where they were hitting.
And that must have been where Foxtrot was, or up in
that area, because they were hitting just on the crest, or
just below the crest, of one of those fingers.

As Echo Company continued to get closer to Foxtrot, they continued to be harassed by NVA troops and also saw increasing signs of their recent presence. Bomb craters and other defensible terrain features were stacked full with NVA weapons and ammunition, staged there so that the attacking NVA could resupply and rearm.

Sergeant Dale Dye: It was hard to see anything, and they had us on line for some reason. Or at least they had my platoon on line. I presume the whole company was. For the first time we began to see where the rounds were hitting. And then we began to see some people. That must have been Fox because they were Marines. I had a bunch of 60-mm mortar rounds, and I think there was a whole bunch of extra machine gun ammo and shit that they took off the tanks. Anyway, we were all loaded down with extra ammunition. We were heavy, not that we weren't usually heavy anyway. We were heavy going up. As we moved up, we were getting hit. The first I remember was we got hit on our right, to my right, and then the next thing I knew, we got hit on our left. Well my platoon got committed, got turned, to the right. So we started sweeping in a westerly direction. But as I understood it, we were no longer tied in with another platoon of ours that was sweeping east. So we were split. I have no idea what happened with the east-bound guys. And I'm not sure that's true, but my platoon was sort of in the center and nobody was behind us. So we started moving to the west and we were sort of on a slope. In other words, we had started up a slope, and we had turned westerly. Now we had some people up high and some people down low; we were on this kind of slope. We started running into these holes. The area had been hit, clearly. I don't know if it had been air strikes or what, but there were a lot of holes and that sort of shit. And there was NVA gear and shit around them. So clearly they had used them at some point for something, whether it was a staging area or what.

20 | FOXTROT'S FINAL MOMENTS ON THE RIDGE

The napalm appeared to have been totally successful in eliminating those NVA soldiers massing at the base of the ridge and posing the immediate threat. The Crow's Nest's desultory fire, largely with AK-47s and RPD machine guns, prevented a quick follow-up. Helicopter gunships arrived at about the same time, strafing and rocketing NVA troops in the near distance and prevented them from joining the battle. There was only the occasional gunshot as the Marines sparingly used their last few precious rounds at targets about which they were certain of success.

FOXTROT RIDGE

PFC Dave Kinsella: There was one fellow who had spotted some gooks down in the tree line, sort of on the southwest, down the hill. Towards the tip of the ridge there was a clump of trees down in there and somebody had spotted some gooks in there. There was one guy firing an M-79 down there, firing grenades down into that tree line. But after that it was pretty much calm. We had the ridge back. It was just Hueys and Phantoms and so on working out around the area there.

Lieutenant Dito went a few yards down the ridge, back to where he had begun the night, to his little command post. That western portion of the ridge had not been as badly ravaged by the flames. He reclaimed his pack unburned but discovered its contents were nonetheless useless to him.

2nd Lieutenant Ray Dito: My pack was stuck out there (near the LZ) and I picked it up the next morning. A couple of weeks before, I received a 'care package' from home and in it were two large salamis. My dad, being Italian, knew that I liked them so he sent me a couple of them. They weighed about a pound apiece and I had shared one of them with some members of the company and also with Major Gagliardo, the Battalion XO. He rated it 'excellent salami.' Anyway, I still had one in my pack, and the next morning when I went back to my pack, that salami had more holes in it than Swiss cheese. It had been riddled. It was just amazing.

Staggering back into the main perimeter from the western finger area came an amazing sight: HM2 "Doc" Sarwicki, who had been shot point-blank in the head while rendering first aid to his wounded Marines. He stumbled toward the Marines' line, having spent the entire night lying among the dead while the NVA roamed that end of the ridge.

Corporal Dave Smith: I saw him the next morning when he came back up then. I hope by now he's okay, but he was a basket case right there, which anybody would be. He was a little, what would you call it? Psychotic? I hope and I pray that it was just at that point.

2nd Lieutenant Ray Dito: It actually hit him on the eye socket bone above his eye. That's where the wound was. The angle of the penetration, whether it was caused by the helmet or just what, it caromed off that bone. It opened up that side of his head, but he didn't lose his eye and didn't penetrate the skull and he survived. He was walking and talking, he was babbling a bit, but he was alive.

Only a short while later, perhaps 20 minutes after the napalm attack, the first elements of Echo Company reached

Foxtrot's defensive perimeter. The Marines of Foxtrot happily greeted them and watched them help reclaim the ridge and pursue the NVA.

2nd Lieutenant Ray Dito: When we moved back into our positions there, that's about the time Echo moved in with us. I was with Captain Russell [CO of Echo Company] at that point. He had moved one of his platoons up into where 1st Platoon was near the edge of the LZ. I remember listening to him, and he gave the order to one of his platoon commanders, 'Clean out that section of the ridge! Assault that section of the ridge!' That was the order that he gave them. I guess there was still a few NVA holed up in some of those holes down there, and so they swept across there through the LZ.

Lance Corporal Robert Kincaid: When Echo came up, they advanced by grenades. They pulled up to our position. Two or three guys pulled up to my left and knelt down, facing the mailbags. I told them I was sure glad to see them up there. 'Sure glad to see you guys.' And he says, 'Well we're going to get you guys out of here. We're going to help you out.' Then he and his partners threw a handful of grenades out in front of them and rushed forward and started doing a fire team rush, toward the mailbags. Kohler and I stood up to move to another position because they were in my direct field of fire, right in front of me, so I was of absolutely no use there. Kohler picked up the M-60 and I got the shotgun, turned to my left and caught a bullet in my right thigh. I got hit between my right knee and buttock.

PFC Dale Braden: One of the guys from Echo come by, and I said, 'Hey, you got any water in your canteen? You know, mine all got burned up and blown up.' And he gave me a drink of his water. Then they swept up toward the Crow's Nest and he got killed. I was still sitting there, and they brought him back to the aid station there and laid him down and I recognized him. I never knew the man's name or nothing but it dawned

on me that, 'One minute you're here and the next
minute you're gone.'

The Marines of Foxtrot Company were covered with the
ashy residue of the napalm strike and splattered with blood,
some from their own wounds and others from the blood of
their friends or the NVA soldiers they had killed at close
range. Sergeant McCoy, bleeding from multiple bullet and
shrapnel wounds, recalls Echo's arrival.

Sergeant Dave McCoy: I was in pretty bad shape. I can
remember when Echo Company came over; they came
over the steep side. That was the only way that they
could come in there without really catching a lot of
flak. I was still conscious when the first guy from Echo
Company came over that hill. I was still conscious
when that went on. At that point I figured we were
pretty much relieved. I looked around and saw a lot of
dead people.
   Everybody up there was black. Everybody had that
napalm, and where it was burning everybody was
filthy, dirty. When these bright white faces from Echo
Company came up that side, to me they had the
whitest, shiniest faces.

Many of the Marines from Echo Company were surprised
that there were so few Foxtrot Marines. Where was the main
body of Foxtrot Company? They had no way of knowing that
most of Foxtrot Company was either dead or wounded by that
time in the battle.

Sergeant Dale Dye: As we continued to move, the
group forward of me made contact with Foxtrot. At
this point, we halted. Then the people on my right
moved around and now we were kind of on the hill
mass. Off to the east of us, or behind us, me and two
other guys—there were two 60-mm mortar guys I was
with—we spotted some movement down below the
hill.
   What I remember in particular was that, you know, I
was looking for Foxtrot. These guys were supposed to
be devilishly in trouble and, more importantly, I wanted

to unload this extra ammo I was carrying. We saw a few of them but, where was the main body of these people?

The Marines of Foxtrot, covered in blood and ash, continued to survey the desolate scene that surrounded them, glad for the arrival of Echo Company. Foxtrot's Marines looked at the death they had wrought and asked one another about the fate of their friends in other squads or other platoons on the ridge.

1st Lieutenant James Jones: I remember a North Vietnamese officer who was killed up there on the ridge, very close to my position. I think he was a captain. All of his gear was new. The contents of his pack were very much like ours. I mean they were different, but he had pictures of his family, new uniforms, and new canteens, and rice bowls and a hammock, one of these green hammocks that they carried. He was roughly a little older than I was and you kind of put yourself in a different position, but he could have easily been you, you know.

Sergeant Joseph Quinn: The whole time I was over there I was only separated for that one day from Bill Grist. I think God wanted me somewhere else. Our hole was somewhere in the middle, near the middle of 1st Platoon, pretty much at the extreme end of the finger. That's where Grist was. During the end of the battle I was asking, 'How's the Bear?' They said, 'He got up, raised his head out of the hole and was shot. He was shot in the head.'

The Marines of Echo Company continued moving over the ridge, walking down into the saddle and then up onto the Crow's Nest.

PFC Chris Gentry: When they came up there, Larry Arthur was laying on the front of the foxhole, of our foxhole. I had my New Testament laying there that had gone through World War I with my grandfather and World War II with my father. They said, 'You guys pack

up and get out of here,' and we literally took off running to get back to the company position.

The Marines on the Crow's Nest hurriedly departed back
down the trail they had climbed less than 24 hours ago. PFC
Blunk, too, was happy to leave and quickly returned to the
ridge below. A few minutes later, though, he remembered that
he had left his pack and other belongings back up on the
Crow's Nest. He sprinted back to gather up his belongings and
then just as hurriedly departed again, this time saying goodbye
forever to the Crow's Nest.

With the arrival of Echo Company, the area was for the
first time secure enough to permit helicopters to land. At long
last, Foxtrot Company would be able to land medevac helicopters and evacuate their critically wounded. The Marines of
Foxtrot gathered their dead comrades and wrapped them in
ponchos before laying them in line near the command post.
They also gathered their wounded near the LZ in anticipation
of their medical evacuation. Lieutenant Jones spoke briefly to
each of the wounded Marines. One of them was Corporal
Howell.

Corporal Kevin "Canadian" Howell: I remember
Lieutenant Jones coming over and looking at me. I had
bandages all over my face and some on my chest. My
uniform, the legs were fairly well burned. He came over
and he knelt down and he said, 'Who is this?' And I tried
to talk to him and he says, 'Is there anything I can do for
you?' I tried to talk and I couldn't. My jaw was broke
and I had a bandage inside my mouth and outside. I'd
been bayoneted in the face; the tip of it broke off.

PFC Kevin Henry: I remember getting medevacced out
and seeing Moses' body. And that shook me up. I had
caught something in the face, around my eye and the
nose. I really didn't want to get medevacced out, but
they sent me out anyhow.

Sergeant Dave McCoy: I think there were nine of us
that they medevacced out on that first Sea Knight
[CH46 Helicopter] that came in there. And I can remem-

ber seeing holes ripped through the side of that as we were taking off, and I said, 'Oh shit, been through all of this and get shot down in a helicopter!'

Lance Corporal Mylin, too, was medevacced out. Within moments he found himself in the battalion aid station, being treated by medical personnel. Most distressing to him, though, was the sight of the badly wounded Sergeant McCoy, who looked like he might not survive his multiple wounds.

Lance Corporal Steve Mylin: The hero that comes to mind that night is McCoy. It was his second tour in 'Nam. He hated it back in the States. He made Sergeant and he was busted. He was really just a cool guy. He was quiet and never loud or bragging, or anything like that. Just a good leader. I can remember him coming around to all of our holes, encouraging us and telling us to 'hang in there' and everything. I knew he got hit really bad that night. He got hit a couple of times. I know he got hit by a rocket, and I'm sure he got hit more than once. When they evacuated me, we were in the same battalion aid station. But McCoy, he looked like he was dead. He had so many bandages on him and he was unconscious; he had all these IVs running into him. He was bandaged head to toe.

With the wounded, some 44 Foxtrot Marines, safely mede-vacced out by helicopter, the 30 or so remaining Marines were told to "saddle up" in preparation to leave Foxtrot Ridge. "Saddling up" was as easy as it could be for the Marines of Foxtrot Company; they had nothing left, only the weapons in their hands. Even the Marines up in the Crow's Nest had very little to carry, since most of them had left their packs and other personal items back down on the ridge. When they came back down, they found everything destroyed.

Sergeant Hubert "Dick" Pressler: I know that when everybody walked off of Foxtrot Ridge, they walked off with what they had on their body when we first origi-nally got burned. We didn't have any extra ammo; we didn't have nothing.

PFC Dave Kinsella: I can remember when Echo came up. We were all just kind of hanging around at that point, at least I was. I remember going off the ridge and I remember all I had was my rifle at the time.

The exhausted Marines of Foxtrot Company filed down off the ridge, crossed Route 9 and ascended a small plateau just to the north of the road. Most of them wandered in a rather stunned silence, gathering together with their friends in little groups of three or four. Some boxes of C rations were brought out, and they ate without real appetite. Someone at LZ Hawk, probably the Battalion Commander, had located an old can of shrimps and sent it out as well.

Sergeant Joseph Quinn: I remember they brought in a can of shrimp, like from World War II, the old shrimp. There was a captain there and he mixed up everything. He said, 'Give me your cheese, give me this and that.' He whipped it all up and that was the best shrimp I ever had in my life. Everybody got two. They were little baby shrimp but they were delicious.

Sergeant Quinn was detailed to locate and guide back a nearby Marine unit that would stand guard in the area. It then began to drizzle with rain and the temperature quickly dropped.

Sergeant Joseph Quinn: They told me and three or four other guys, we had to bring another platoon that were maybe a couple hundred yards away. We had to go find them. They were up the road in a tree line. It was pitch dark. We walked right up in the CP. We were standing there, and we heard them talking amongst themselves. I ask, 'Is Lieutenant so and so here?' And he said, 'Yeah, right here,' and so I said, We're here to guide you back.' He said, 'How the hell did you get in here?'

I remember sleeping in the hole. It was raining, drizzling. We slept in the holes and we wrapped ourselves in newspaper because all our shirts—well, my shirt— was burned up. I just had a green T-shirt. I wrapped up in newspapers, and I remember laying there and I'm thinking, 'Hey, these bums don't have it too bad.'

Laying in the bottom of the hole with newspapers, and I was warm.

Lance Corporal Doug "Deuce" Near: I remember walking off that ridge and I remember us setting in across the road that day. We had them damn tanks there. And somehow I woke up, and there was a tank backing up towards me. I scrambled my ass out of that tank's way. I thought, 'We just came off this damn ridge, survived it, and I'm going to have an American tank run over my ass!'

PFC Dave Kinsella: We went down to that big flat dirt spot. I think it was right below LZ Hawk and we spent the night there. I know it rained that night. I was laying in a hole and I woke up the next morning, and there was probably about four inches of water in the bottom of that hole, it seemed like. But I know I slept all night, pretty good after being up the night before all night. I laid in the hole; I was right in the bottom.

Sergeant Hubert "Dick" Pressler: I was colder than anything and trying to find something to keep warm. The only way we kept warm that night is about three or four of us got together and we just huddled together.

PFC Chris Gentry: I had no weapon. I had no ammunition. They just told us to stay out here and nobody stayed awake. Every one of us, I believe, went to sleep that night. Laid down in a heap and went to sleep. I wouldn't have cared if they killed me then; it wouldn't have made any difference. Kill me or let me sleep.

The next morning, resupplies came in for the Marines of Foxtrot Company: weapons, ammunition, canteens, cartridge belts, clothing. They needed, and were supplied with, everything.

1st Lieutenant James Jones: Once we got off the hill, the first order of business was to resupply the company. We had no clothes, people had no packs, and we had no ammunition except for the AK-47s and the North

Vietnamese ammunition. I mean, we needed everything. And they did that. The next morning they came
out, and they gave us the gear that we needed.

The battle of Foxtrot Ridge was over for the Marines of
Foxtrot Company, 2nd Battalion, 3rd Marine Regiment. They
had suffered 13 killed and 44 wounded but had managed to
stave off a North Vietnamese Army force that outnumbered
them by more than ten to one. For those Marines not wounded
in the battle, the war continued for them as before. Some of the
wounded returned to the war, trickling back singly or in little
groups of two or three in the following days and weeks. Many
of the wounded never returned; their injuries were too severe.
While some of the Marines of Foxtrot received medals for their
valor and the unit would be praised for its courage and pro-
fessionalism, probably the greatest recognition bestowed upon
them by their fellow Marines was the dubbing of that previously unnamed piece of real estate forevermore in U.S. Marine
Corps history as "Foxtrot Ridge."

EPILOGUE

Pitched battles continued on Foxtrot Ridge for days after Foxtrot 2/3 left the ridge on May 28, 1968. For several days afterwards, there were countless acts of heroism and sacrifice on the part of other Marines who had taken over the ridge's defenses. On the evening of May 28, while Foxtrot Company was settled into their barren plot of red earth a few kilometers away, just north of Route 9, Echo Company now occupied Foxtrot Ridge and would see its own fierce fighting there.

At approximately 8:50 PM on May 28, their first night on the ridge, Echo Company was hit by 25 rounds of 60-mm mortar fire but miraculously took no casualties. The next day, Echo began sighting NVA troops in the distance. At 2:20 PM, they spotted three NVA soldiers walking across the crest of a small hill, which the Marines happened to use as a "registration point" for their artillery. They were thus able to fire an immediate and precisely accurate barrage onto the unlucky NVA, killing them immediately. The Marines did the same some 40 minutes later, this time causing a large "secondary explosion" as the NVA soldiers' own ammunition exploded and added to the blast. As evening approached, the NVA retaliated with five 82-mm mortar rounds of their own, wounding three Echo Company Marines.

On the night of May 30, the NVA struck the Marines holding Foxtrot Ridge again. In a ground assault, which continued throughout the night and the early morning hours of May 31, the Marines of Echo Company suffered 4 killed and 48 wounded, halving their strength at the cost of 64 NVA soldiers killed in the battle. Captain William Russell was badly wounded in the action but refused to concede and continued to lead his men in the battle.

This time it was Foxtrot's turn to come to the aid of Echo. A platoon (now down to a dozen men) from Foxtrot accompanied the two tanks from LZ Hawk to a position northwest of the ridge and fired at NVA soldiers attempting to flee from Echo Company's defense of Foxtrot Ridge and escape to Laos. By the evening of May 31, with Echo Company now down to half its strength, it was decided to reinforce them with Golf Company. At 5:40 PM, Golf Company arrived at Foxtrot Ridge by helicopter while the NVA fired ten 82-mm mortars at the Marines in reply. One Marine was killed and another two were wounded in the action. The combined force of Golf and Echo Companies would remain together on the ridge for several more days. While mortar and artillery fire was occasionally exchanged, it became clear that the NVA had given up on dislodging the Marines. The Marines had proven their point: if they wanted to hold the ridge, they could. The Marines, however lacked the manpower to keep troops emplaced on every piece of high ground. Furthermore, the ridge's value to the Marines lay primarily in its use as a platform from which to kill NVA soldiers. Once the NVA withdrew from the fight, it lost that value and the Marines of Echo and Golf Companies were required in other contested areas.

However, that wasn't the end of the blood shed on Foxtrot Ridge. In late June 1968, elements of the 3rd and the 11th Engineer Battalions, as well as the 3rd Shore Party Battalion, were busy using bulldozers to dismantle the soon-to-be-abandoned base at Khe Sanh. To protect their southern flank and prevent NVA troops from hindering their efforts, India Company, 3rd Battalion, 4th Marine Regiment, commanded by Captain Merlyn Sexton, was sent to occupy Foxtrot Ridge. At 3:00 AM on July 1, the NVA began a series of probing attacks against India Company. Then, at 7:30 AM, the NVA launched a full-scale attack while NVA mortars and 130-mm artillery hammered the Marines on Foxtrot Ridge. The Marines were able to blunt the attack, killing more than 100 NVA soldiers at the cost of two Marines killed. The rest of the NVA unit withdrew, but they were later spotted by the Marines as they attempted to withdraw into Laos. The Marines hit them with helicopter gunships and fixed-wing airstrikes, bringing the NVA losses to 203 killed in the engagement.

Foxtrot Ridge, as it was known after Foxtrot 2/3's epic battle of May 28, was thus also the scene of bloody battles involving Echo 2/3, Golf 2/3, and India 3/4. For an obscure and otherwise unremarkable plot of ground, Foxtrot Ridge was the scene of immense courage and carnage from May 1968 through July 1968.

APPENDIX A

THE MARINES OF FOXTROT COMPANY, 2ND BATTALION, 3RD MARINE REGIMENT, 3RD MARINE DIVISION CITED IN FOXTROT RIDGE

PFC Laurence Kenneth Arthur: Laurence Arthur was killed in action in South Vietnam on May 28, 1968. He was 18 years old.

Lance Corporal Moses June Bacote: Moses Bacote was killed in action in South Vietnam on May 28, 1968. He was 22 years old.

Corporal Steven Dewitt Baker: Steven Baker was killed in action in South Vietnam on May 28, 1968. He was 22 years old.

PFC Harold Blunk: After Vietnam and his subsequent discharge, Harold Blunk left the Marine Corps and became successful in business. For several years he owned and managed a resort hotel in St Croix. He is currently planning a trip back to Vietnam and hopes to revisit Foxtrot Ridge and the Crow's Nest.

PFC Dale Braden: Dale Braden completed his tour in Vietnam, then went to Camp Pendleton, and then to Hawaii as an MP. He was discharged in 1971 and returned to his hometown in Missouri. He works for the City of Poplar Bluff, is married and has two children, a daughter aged 25 and a son aged 30.

Lance Corporal Jim Chafin: Jim Chafin was wounded three different times in Vietnam. He married his high school sweetheart, Sandy, in January 1969 and left the Marines in September 1969. He has been married for 32 years, has a son aged 23 and a daughter aged 26. ('I remember thoughts while I was on Foxtrot Ridge. I had dated my high school sweetheart and we were engaged when I went to Vietnam. I can't tell you how many times that night I thought about her. I was just lucky to get home and be with her.')

Lance Corporal Curtis "Snake" Clark: Curtis Clark completed his tour in Vietnam and eventually left the Marines after 10 years in 1977. He is now in senior management in the computer industry and lives in Atlanta, Georgia. He maintains contact with his best friend Robert Croft who served with him in Vietnam.

PFC Robert "Hillbilly" Croft: Robert Croft completed his tour of duty in Vietnam and served briefly at Camp Lejeune before signing a waiver and returning to Foxtrot Company for his second tour of duty in Vietnam. When the 3rd Marine Regiment withdrew from Vietnam, he was transferred to Echo 2/5 and in the tenth month of his second tour was critically wounded and medevacced eventually to a Naval Hospital in Japan. Once his wounds healed, he was assigned to the 1st Marine Air Wing as sergeant of the guard at the base there in Okinawa. When his four-year enlistment was up, he was discharged at the rank of sergeant. Robert Croft now lives with his family in Tennessee.

Lance Corporal Richard "Dickie" Cutbirth: Richard Cutbirth was killed in action in South Vietnam on May 28, 1968. He was 19 years old.

Lance Corporal Michael John Cutri: Michael Cutri was killed in action in South Vietnam on May 28, 1968. He was 18 years old.

2nd Lieutenant Ray Dito: Ray Dito completed his tour in Vietnam and, upon discharge from the Marines, returned to his native San Francisco area. He is a Captain in the Fire Department and is married with three children.

Sergeant Dale Dye: Dale Dye stayed in the Marines and became an officer. He retired as a captain and now works in Hollywood as a technical advisor to the film industry. His credits include Saving Private Ryan and Platoon.

PFC Chris Gentry: Chris Gentry did a second tour of duty with the 3rd Battalion, 9th Marines. ("When I came back from that I thought, 'My gosh I've had two tours of this and I know just about everything I ever want to know about combat and carrying a pack and a rifle'.") Chris became an intelligence analyst and was then selected for Warrant Officer. He progressed through the Warrant ranks and later became a commissioned officer. He eventually retired from the Marines and now works in the construction business. He and his wife recently celebrated their 32nd wedding anniversary. They have one son and two grandchildren. (When asked about his deeds on Foxtrot Ridge, he replied: "I was just an average guy then and I'm an average guy now.")

Lance Corporal William "the Bear" Grist: William Grist was killed in action in South Vietnam on May 28, 1968. He was 19 years old.

Lance Corporal Robert "Skip" Hedrick: Skip Hedrick retired from the Marine Corps in 1989 after 22-1/2 years. He achieved the rank of 1st Sergeant. He lives with his wife and family in Montana.

PFC Kevin Henry: Kevin Henry left the Marines soon after completing his tour in Vietnam and began a long and successful career in the automobile business. He lives in Teaneck, New Jersey. ("There haven't been a whole lot of days in the past 30 years that I haven't thought about Dickie Cutbirth. We were trained in a very severe school. And as the years have gone by, you begin to appreciate just what a remarkable imprint the Marine Corps makes on a young man or a young woman.")

Corporal Kevin "Canadian" Howell: Kevin Howell's tour in Vietnam ended in October 1968. He said he would only return if he was promised he could serve with Foxtrot 2/3 (He was "only" an attachment on Foxtrot Ridge.). He did complete another tour and stayed in the Marines, eventually retiring as a 1st Sergeant. Kevin Howell met up again with "Lieutenant" (now General) Jones again in 1999. They both recalled those last moments on Foxtrot Ridge before Kevin was medevacced out, and Lieutenant Jones had inquired "Is there anything I can do for you?" Kevin had been unable to speak because of his wounds and broken jaw. "I told him the night he made Commandant, we were in the rose garden drinking beer with him. This was, like two o'clock in the morning. General Jones said, 'What was it you were trying to say, Canadian?' And I said, I was trying to say "Yes, you can. You can get me the fuck out of here!" Kevin Howell lives with his wife (Sharon) and family in North Carolina.

Lance Corporal Randy Huber: Randy Huber was killed in action in South Vietnam on May 28, 1968. He was 19 years old.

1st Lieutenant James Jones: Jim Jones remained in the Marines and is now General James Jones, Commandant of the Marine Corps. He lives with his wife and family in Washington, D.C. When he was installed as Commandant in 1999, he invited those who had served with him in Foxtrot 2/3 as his special guests at the festivities.

Lance Corporal Gary Lyle Kestler: Gary Kestler was killed in action in South Vietnam on May 28, 1968. He was 20 years old.

Lance Corporal Robert Kincaid: Robert Kincaid was wounded on Foxtrot Ridge and sent to "Charlie Med" at Phu Bai. ("I was there at Charlie Med for a week, maybe, and then back to the company. It was a 'through-and-through,' a flesh wound.") After completing his tour in Vietnam and subsequently leaving the Marines, he worked in the steel industry for some years. He graduated from Northeastern University in Boston and was a Department of Defense Special Agent in Washington until he retired in 1989. Now an ordained minister, Robert Kincaid counsels veterans and runs a horse and cattle ranch in Montana.

PFC Dave Kinsella: Dave Kinsella completed his tour in Vietnam, left the Marines, and lives in South Carolina. He has had a long and successful career in industry, still enjoys hunting and fishing, and also runs a thriving part-time business in the taxidermy trade.

Corporal Gary "Tex" La Bonte: Gary La Bonte survived Foxtrot Ridge. In a subsequent engagement, he was killed in action in South Vietnam on July 17, 1968. He was 20 years old.

Gunnery Sergeant Ralph Larsen: Ralph Larsen eventually retired from the Marines as a Sergeant Major. His now lives in Florida and is a postal worker.

Corporal Ron "Pappy" Lockley: Ron Lockley stayed in the Marines for nine and a half years. He completed a second tour of duty in Vietnam and was discharged as a Staff Sergeant. He lives with his wife (Joy) and nine-year-old son (Alex) in North Carolina. ("There have been very few days since that I have not thought about the guys we lost that night. We lost a good part of our platoon.")

Lance Corporal Ralph Joseph Luebbers, Jr.: Ralph Luebbers was killed in action in South Vietnam on May 28, 1968. He was 21 years old.

PFC Woodrow Makin, Jr.: Woodrow Makin was killed in action in South Vietnam on May 28, 1968. He was 20 years old.

Sergeant Dave McCoy: Dave McCoy was badly wounded on Foxtrot Ridge and medevacced to Dong Ha, and then to the hospital ship, USS Repose, and to Great Lakes Naval Hospital. When he was finally released, he left the Marine Corps and returned to his work as a carpenter. He now lives in Las Vegas, Nevada.

Lance Corporal Steve Mylin: Steve Mylin was wounded on Foxtrot Ridge and sent to a hospital in Japan. He never returned to Vietnam. He remarried several years ago and has three children: ages, 4, 8, and 12. ("I still consider myself a Marine. I get Leatherneck and Gazette. The Marine Corps is still very much a part of my life.")

Lance Corporal Doug "Deuce" Near: Doug Near "extended" and served an additional three months in Vietnam. He later left the Marines and joined the Navy, retiring eventually from the Navy in 1999. He now works as a prisons officer in Illinois. ("We did a lot of growing up that night. Things got put in perspective real quick. I have probably relived segments of that fight on a monthly basis. It just sticks with you.")

PFC Mike Nichols: Mike Nichols left the Marines soon after returning from Vietnam. He has been in the trucking business for the past 25 years. He has lived in eastern Kentucky since 1969. He is married to Sandy and has two children, a daughter (Deanna) and a son (David).

Lance Corporal Stanley Poniktera, Jr.: Stanley Poniktera was killed in action in South Vietnam on May 28, 1968. He was 18 years old.

Sergeant Hubert "Dick" Pressler: Dick Pressler spent 27 years in the Marine Corps and retired in 1988 as a Master Gunnery Sergeant. He lives in North Carolina.

Sergeant Joseph Quinn: Joe Quinn left the Marines shortly after his tour in Vietnam and joined the Abington, Pennsylvania, Police Department, retiring as a Lieutenant. He now works as a traffic safety manager. He and wife (Nancy) have three children and five grandchildren. He asked specifically that those killed on Foxtrot Ridge be remembered, especially his good friends, Bill Grist, Michael Smith, and Steven Baker. ("A lot of my squad was killed. That's why I think God wanted me out of there for the night.")

PFC Lorcin "Chico" Rodriguez: Enquiries indicate that Chico Rodriguez completed his tour of duty in Vietnam and left the Marines. He died in the mid-1980s.

HM2 Frank Sarwiki: Frank Sarwicki is believed to have passed away in the early 1980s.

Private Donald Philip Schuck: Donald Schuck was killed in action in South Vietnam on May 28, 1968. He was 18 years old.

Corporal Dave Smith: Dave Smith left the Marines when his enlistment was up and worked for a while as a cowboy. He later became a teacher and has taught high school for the past 27 years. He is also a football and swimming coach. Dave Smith specifically asked that the Marines of Whisky Battery be remembered. He also asked that two individuals be singled out for acknowledgement: the corpsman who was with 2nd Platoon, Tom Jones, and one of the gunners back in the 81s Platoon: Lance Corporal Tim Alexander. ("He was one of them firing at LZ Hawk.")

Lance Corporal Michael "Smitty" Smith: Michael Smith was killed in action in South Vietnam on May 28, 1968. He was 20 years old.

2nd Lieutenant William Tehan: Bill Tehan served a second tour of duty in Vietnam and was wounded a total of seven times. The bullet holes in his head have filled with calcium deposits, and the bullet fragments remain hidden from view. There is little evidence of the wound today. He retired from the Marines in 1991 as a Lieutenant Colonel. He now works for the Defense Intelligence Agency in Washington, D.C. Bill Tehan is married with two children. Recently he and his wife were shopping at a carpet store where Bill thought he recognized the owner as a former Marine. When they established that they had both served in the same unit, the owner (Louis Miccio) remarked, "Do you remember seeing that red-headed lieutenant and seeing an NVA put a gun to his head and blow him away?" Bill Tehan responded, "Well, get ready for this, I was that Lieutenant." Louis Miccio had assumed all these years that the lieutenant had died, and now felt he had been "witness to a miracle."

Lance Corporal Alan "Chief" Walker: Alan Walker left the Marines soon after returning from Vietnam. He lives in Nebraska with his wife and family and is actively involved in the Native American community there.

PFC Mark Woodruff: Mark Woodruff completed his tour in Vietnam and left the Marines in late 1969. He completed his university studies in psychology and emigrated to Australia in the early 1970s. He works there as a psychologist and is a Lieutenant Commander in the Royal Australian Navy Reserve. He also has written extensively about the Vietnam War.

APPENDIX B

SOURCES

All information contained in this book is based upon the following interviews by the author (their source clearly identifiable in the text) unless otherwise referenced:

Blunk, Harold: December 4, 2000

Chafin, Jim: May 24, 2001

Clark, Curtis: August 3, 2001

Croft, Robert: January 29, 2001

Dishman, Lieutenant Colonel Wilbur, USMC
    (Ret): January 12, 2001

Dito, Ray: February 1, 2001

Dye, Captain Dale, USMC (Ret): January 6, 2001

Gentry, Captain Reuben, USMC
    (Ret): March 22, 2001 and March 25, 2001

Hedrick, 1st Sergeant Robert, USMC
    (Ret): February 25, 2001

Henry, Kevin: April 3, 2001

Howell, 1st Sergeant Kevin, USMC (Ret): June 2, 2001

Jones, General James L., USMC: January 12, 2001

Kinkaid, Robert: February 2, 2001

Kinsella, Dave: October 17, 2001

Larsen, Sergeant Major Ralph, USMC
    (Ret): January 7, 2001

Lockley, Ron: January 29, 2001

Martin, Lieutenant Colonel Justin, USMC
    (Ret): October 15, 2000

McCoy, Dave: March 25, 2001

Mylin, Steve: January 6, 2001

Near, Doug: February 6, 2001

Nichols, Mike: February 20, 2001

Pressler, Master Gunnery Sergeant Hubert, USMC
    (Ret): April 24, 2001

Quinn, Joseph: January 4, 2001

Smith, Dave: November 12, 2000

Tehan, Lieutenant Colonel William, USMC
    (Ret): January 17, 2001

Walker, Alan: December 30, 2000

Woodruff, Mark: February 13, 2001

APPENDIX C

ADDITIONAL EXPLANATORY CHAPTER NOTES

Chapter One

The figures for killed in action (KIA) and wounded in action (WIA) were taken from the *Command Chronology for the Second Battalion, Third Marine Regiment* (henceforth referred to as "*Command Chronology*") for January, February, March, and April 1968.

The "Blooded and well oiled machine" quote is from the Colonel Jack Davis memo of 26 Jan 1968.

Chapter Two

Some uncertainty remains about how the three platoons were deployed. It is clear that 1st Platoon had the western "finger," and 2nd Platoon had that area facing the Crow's Nest. Several of those interviewed, including platoon leaders, recall 3rd Platoon being "split" (because of the narrow perimeter) and covering the middle of the ridge on both the northern and southern slopes. This would have been a most unusual deployment. Because of this uncertainty and because it doesn't play any real role in the battle except that of a historical curiosity, I have kept to a description of the defense by referring to sections of the ridge rather than platoons for the most part.

Chapter Six

The precise times of these actions are uncertain. They are not logged with any real accuracy into the *Command Chronology* which is intended to be more of a "large-scale and general" picture of activities. Often, whole hours of fighting are condensed in the *Command Chronologies* under one description. Times throughout are based on a consensus of those interviewed.

Chapter Eight

Much confusion remains about the color of the flare used to launch the attack. The memories of those who were there are split fairly equally between remembering that it was launched with a red and countered by a green, or launched by a green and countered by a red. I should also point out that the sky was filled with green (NVA) and red (Marine) tracers. The significance of those two small flares was lost in the "pyrotechnic psychosis" those on Foxtrot Ridge underwent for the next several hours. In the past, I have believed and written that it was launched with a green flare. In speaking with "Gunny" Larsen, however, whose memory of this is crystal clear and whose Korean War experiences make it so logical to have fired a green flare to stop an attack, I have changed my mind about what probably took place. Also, in an oral history taken a few days after the battle by USMC oral historians, 1st Lieutenant Jones is quoted as saying it was started with a red flare and the Marines responded with a green flare. (*Interview with 1st Lieutenant James Jones at LZ Hawk, May 28-29, 1968*, Tape 2745, Oral History, Headquarters USMC.). So, I think the weight of evidence supports the account I give in this book. Where this differs from their comments to me in interview, I have placed the color of the flare in brackets.

I go on about this in such detail, mainly out of a desire for historical accuracy, but also to explain to those who recalled it differently, why I have written the account the way I have. Really, though, it makes no significant difference. The important point is that the NVA launched the attack with a colored flare and the Marines responded with the "opposite" color, confusing the enemy.

Chapter Ten

The account of Lance Corporal Luebers' actions are from Alan "Chief" Walker. He was told of this a short time after the battle by one of the two Marines (PFC Jacebo) whom Lance Corporal Luebers threw into the foxhole and then shielded with his own body. Both of these Marines survived the battle, although their whereabouts today are unknown.

Chapter Eleven

The account of HM2 Frank 'Doc' Sarwicki is from *HM2 Emanual Layos Interview at LZ Hawk, May 28-29, 1968*, Tape 2745, Oral History, Headquarters USMC.

Chapter Twelve

The actions of the NVA ("...babbling incoherently," etc.) are from *Interview with 1st Lieutenant James Jones at LZ Hawk, May 28-29, 1968*, Tape 2745, Oral History, Headquarters USMC.

Chapter Twenty

The figure of 13 Marines killed and 44 wounded is from the *Command Chronology*. That chronology also notes that 230 dead NVA were counted on the battlefield around Foxtrot Ridge. "Intercepts" of NVA radio communications later established that NVA forces had committed four battalions to the attack, but because of the small size of the battlefield, could commit only two battalions (800-1000 men) at a time. Eventually, after Foxtrot had been relieved by Echo and Golf Companies, the NVA committed a fifth battalion. These same radio intercepts indicate that the NVA Regimental Commander was killed and that one NVA battalion essentially "ceased to exist." This information is from an unnamed but reliable source. It is currently the subject of a Freedom of Information (FOI) request I have filed with the National Security Agency (NSA) and the U.S. Marine Corps.

APPENDIX D

COMMAND CHRONOLOGY
2ND BATTALION, 3RD MARINE REGIMENT
MAY, 1968

The following documents are extracts from the Command Chronology for 2/3 which records the battalion's activities during the month of May 1968. The six numbers at the left provide the date and time of the event. The first two numbers are the date and the next four are the time, using the military '24 hour' clock. Thus, the first entry reads '222345H' and means this occurred on May 22 at 2345 hours (or 11:45 PM). The grid coordinates (eg 'XD 864404') refer to the military maps then in use. Probably the most significant of these is the ridge located at 'XD874383' which would become known as Foxtrot Ridge.

222345H CoE received 4 rounds of rifle grenades south of defensive position and replied with 81mm mortar fire.

231015H CoF vicinity XD 861398 observed enemy artillery rounds impacting vicinity XD 864404 from an estimated azimuth of 4200 mils from friendly position.

241255H CoF vicinity XD 869398 received 7 artillery rounds from CoRoc and called in a 155mm counterbattery mission from K.S.

241305H CoG vicinity XD 884386 took incoming Chicom grenades and replied with 60mm fire and continued the attack.

241400H CoG vicinity XD 884385 while sweeping from vicinity XD 884385 to XD 889380 received Chicom grenades and heavy small arms fire from an estimated company of NVA. The enemy was well dug in in spider traps and bunkers extending along the ridge line. Enemy positions withstood prep fire by air and artillery. After the initial contact the enemy attempted to flank friendly positions. CoG returned fire with small arms, M-60, M-79 and 60mm fire. AO and gunships called on station followed by fixed wing strikes. Action resulted in 12 USMC KIA, 17 USMC WIA and 2 NVA KIA.

241800H CoG vicinity XD 884385 and XD 885384 pulled back from objective after earlier action and called in 2 flights of fixed wing aircraft, artillery and 81mm mortar fire. Resumed attack and received heavy volume of small arms and automatic weapons fire from enemy dug in on objective. Gunships, M-60 machine-guns, 60mm and 81mm mortars and artillery fired on enemy positions and covered evacuation of WIA, resulting in 3 USMC KIA, 4 USMC WIA, 30 NVA KIA.

242015H CoG vicinity XD 8822382 secured high ground when heavily camaflaged NVA in spider traps in dense underbrush opened fire. 60mm and 81mm mortars, gunships and artillery plus air strikes were employed. Results: 10 NVA KIA, 15 USMC KIA, and 21 USMC WIA.

250035H CoH vicinity of Bridge #34, XD 914403. Took 3 Chicom grenades into defense perimeter. Called in night defensive fire. 2 USMC WIANE.

250600H CoG vicinity of XD 888388 received 7 incoming grenades. Returned fire with M-26 grenades and called in illumination. Results negative.

250615H CoG vicinity of XD 888388 while checking area found 1 NVA KIA and 1 AK-47 with 3 magazines.

UNCLASSIFIED

251940H CP 2dBn, 3dMar vicinity XD 895406 received 6 artillery rounds. Fired 115 105mm Artillery rounds, counterbattery at XD 872354 and XD 872320.

250800H to 251900H CoF vicinity XD 8738 and 8737. During this period of time CoG and CoF continued the attack against an estimated Battalion of NVA, to search out and destroy the enemy and to recover friendly KIA's. Supporting arms were used to prep the objective and air strikes were used. A total of 18 flights of air, 600 rounds of artillery, 500 rounds of 81mm mortars, 50 rounds of 90mm and 28 rounds 106mm were utilized. CoG swept through the objective and recovered friendly KIA's and found NVA KIA's and equipment. AO's on station reported ragged enemy withdrawal to the southand southeast. Many blood trails were noted on objective. CoF and CoG established defensive perimeters and continued to fire artillery and 81mm mortars on suspected enemy locations. Found 32 Chicom grenades, 5 AK-47's, 1 AK-50 machine-gun, 2 Chicom carbines, 6 RPG rounds, 3 helmets, 3 belts, and machine-gun ammunition. Results showed 21 NVA KIA.

260500H CoG vicinity XD 883388 heard heavy movement east of position. Checked at first light and found large amount of bandages and fresh blood. LP used M-26 grenades to cover area of movement.

261100H CoH vicinity XD 866397 friendly artillery hit near tank and engineers on road sweep. Check fire. Investigation being conducted. Resulting in 1 USMC KIA, 4 USMC WIA. Investigation conducted included actual sightings of all friendly rounds, recheck of fire mission from both guns and FO's records. HE rounds fired by artillery were on target. Rounds received were individual, but landed during conduction of mission. Rounds were not friendly as originally suspected. Units should be aware of the enemy's consistent efforts to fire rounds just off our missions in order to confuse and to obtain check fires.

261355H CoG vicinity of XD 7432 received 6 to 7 incoming artillery rounds. Fired 155mm counterbattery at CoRoc. Results show 3 USMC WIA, 2 (major) and 1 (minor).

261510H CP, 2dBn, 3dMar vicinity of XD 8640 and XD 8740 received 7 rounds of artillery fire. Called in 105mm artillery counterbattery.

261730H CoF vicinity XD 861359. Spotted 6 NVA with helmets and packs in open. Called in artillery fire.

UNCLASSIFIED

261905H CoF vicinity XD 861359. Spotted 5 NVA on ridge line with
         packs and helmets. Called in artillery and 2 jet air
         strikes. Al contained 15 fresh overhead bunkers. Re-
         sults show 2 NVA KIA.

261940H CoH vicinity XD 885399 spotted 6 NVA moving west. Fired
         40 rounds of 81mm mortars.

262015H CoF vicinity XD 880372. Spotted 30 NVA moving in column
         accross an open ridge line. Called in artillery and 81mm
         mortar fire. Resulting in scattering the NVA.

262130H CP, 2dBn, 3dMar vicinity XD 94142. spotted enemy gun
         flashes to N.E. Fired 155mm artillery counterbattery in-
         to area.

271230H CoH vicinity XD 806395 conducted search and destroy sweep
         after artillery and air prep of objective area

271240H to 271315H CoG vicinity of XD 863397 received 10 rounds of
         artillery fire. Determined to be from CoRoc. Counterbat-
         tery requested on CoRoc.

271515H CoF vicinity XD 874384 received AO report of results of
         105mm artillery and 81mm fire mission of 262015H vicinity
         XD 880372. AO confirmed 7 NVA KIA.

271725H CoG vicinity XD 865398 received 4 130mm artillery rounds
         from CoRoc. AO, on station, observed firing point.

280245H to 280250H CoF vicinity XD 874383 received enemy probe.
         Initial enemy movement observed by LP using Starlight
         Scope. Night defensive fires called in. Enemy force over-
         ran 4 man LP north of defensive perimeter when 3 NVA jump-
         ed into LP position with satchel charges, killing themsel-
         ves and 3 of the 4 Marines. Enemy assaulted on a wide
         front from north utilizing heavy small arms fire and at
         least 40 RPG rounds. CoF fired the FPL. Enemy utilized
         pencil flares to control their attack. CoF company com-
         mander fired a green pencil flare and enemy momentarily
         broke contact.

280300H CoF vicinity XD 874383 received full scale attack by esti-
         mated NVA Battalion. Enemy used heavy RPG fire to breach
         1st Platoon position and over-run 60mm mortar position.
         2d and 3d Platoons adjusts to form 360 degree defense while
         1st Platoon regroups to establish defensive position on
         knoll to the east of original position. Night defensive
         fire and illumination fired by Battery B, 1/12 and 2dBn,
         3dMar 81mm mortars. NVA using RPG rounds from high ground
         vicinity XD 880383 to support attack.

280325H   CoG vicinity XD 870393 received 40 rounds of 130mm artillery fire from CoRoc.

280330H   CoF vicinity XD 874383. NVA attack slackens and CoG consolidates defensive positions.

280415H   CoF vicinity XD 874383. Flare plane and sixed wing gunship arrive on station. Volumn of NVA fire increases against friendly forces. Enemy .50 Cal machine-gun fires at gunship.

280415H to 280620H   CoF vicinity XD 874383. Heavy contact continues between CoF and estimated NVA Battalion. Enemy continues to attack and regroup attempting to over-run friendly positions with mass ground attack supported by RPG's and automatic fire.

280620H   CoG vicinity XD 870393 received 4 rounds 130mm artillery fire from CoRoc. Results show 4 USMC WIA.

280700H   CoF vicinity XD 874383. Helicopter gunships on station with LO. LO reports that NVA bodies litter area around CoF position. Small groups of enemy continue to fire at friendly positions.

281045H   CoE vicinity XD 870392 moving south from Route #9 to support CoF. 2 tanks in direct support fired 90mm fire on enemy troops moving accross and up ridgeline toward CoF position. Resulting in 4 NVA KIA with 90mm fire.

281130H   CoF vicinity XD 874383. Fixed wing aircraft delivered napalm on ridgeline west of defensive perimeter against NVA reinforcements moving from west and southwest. Napalm hit within 20 meters of friendly lines. Fire, fanned by wind swept CoF positions forcing friendly forces to withdraw from ridgeline. The napalm killed an estimated 30 NVA halted the organized enemy attack. As fire subsided on ridgeline, CoF Marines quickly returned to man defensive positions and pursued by fire as enemy troops withdrew.

281150H   CoE vicinity XD 874383 arrived in support of CoF. Groups of NVA continued to deliver sporadic fire from east and west of CoF position. CoE swept west along ridgeline routing enemy from fighting holes and bomb craters. After securing western portion of ridgeline, CoE commenced sweep to east where 1st Platoon of CoF was receiving enemy fire from high ground to east, southeast and northeast.

UNCLASSIFIED

281355H CoE vicinity XD 876381. AO observed 30 NVA in treeline
below and southeast of CoF. CoE using M-26 grenades and
M-79 grenade launchers took the NVA under fire. AO adjusted rounds, filling and confusing the enemy until the
remaining NVA fled to the south. At 1500H emergency resupply arrived by helo at Co's E and F positions and took
out CoF WIA. CoE continued the attack making use of supporting arms moved to night positions. Results: 13 USMC
KIA, 44 USMC WIA and 176 NVA KIA with many bodies remaining in areas not yet searched. Many weapons and ammunition and documents were found. Report will follow on the
29th of May.

281805H CoH vicinity of XD 907386 received 6 mortar rounds, 82mm.
Called in 105mm artillery conterbattery. 1 USMC WIA.

281825H CoE vicinity of YD 877370 and XD 872380 spotted 4 NVA at
XD 877370 and NVA digging in at XD 872380. Called in artillery fire.

281900H Assumed OpCon CoE, 2dBn, 1stMar.

282000H CP, 2dBn, 3dMar vicinity of XD 895406 received 1 82mm
mortar round. Unable to determine enemy position.

282050H CoE vicinity of XD 870374 received 25 60mm mortar rounds.
Fired artillery counterbattery mission on suspected enemy position.

290430H CoH vicinity XD 89463734 received 5 82mm mortar rounds.
Replied with 105mm artillery counterbattery fire.

290700H CoE, 2dBn, 1stMar to 2dBn, 1stMar.

290900H CoE and CoF vicinity XD 874383 conducted thorough sweep
of area where massive enemy attack occured on 28 May.
Found 54 NVA KIA, 1 .30 Cal heavy machine-gun, 8 AK-50's,
46 AK-47's, 14 AK-47 magazines, 4 SKS, 4 AK-50 drums, 4
RPG rocket launchers, 7 RPG rounds, 8 RPG rocket boosters,
15 Chicom grenades, approximately 2000 rounds of assorted
ammunition and miscellaneous 782 gear, papers and documents. Will forward weapons, papers and documents to S-2.

291420H CoE vicinity XD 874383 observed 3 NVA at XD 872369. Coordinates were known 105mm artillery registration point,
called 105mm fire for effect. Results 3 NVA KIA.

291500H CoE vicinity XD 874383 observed 1 NVA at XD 875359. Called in 105mm artillery mission resulted in secondary explosion.

292230H CoE vicinity XD 874383 received enemy ground probe on west
         side of defensive perimeter. Fired night defensive fires
         with 60mm mortars, 81mm mortars and 105mm artillery. Results
         of fire 1 NVA KIA and captured 3 AK-47's, 1 RPG, 1 ammo drum,
         5 ChiCom grenades and 1 satchel charge.

292300H CoE vicinity XD 874383 3 RPG rounds hit outside of def-
         ensive perimeter. Called 81mm mortar and 105mm artillery
         fire on suspected enemy firing position.

300045H CoE vicinity XD 674382 sighted 2 secondary explosions after
         receiving 1 RPG and 2 grenades and firing an artillery fire
         mission.

300330H CoE vicinity XD 874382 received 2 RPG rounds and replied with
         81mm mortars and artillery.

300740H CoE while searching the area around its defensive position
         found 1 new NVA helmet and a fresh trail of blood attributed
         to night defensive fires.

300940H CoE vicinity XD 874382 observed 2 UH1E gunships receive fire
         from vicinity XD 872368. Gunships returned fire and CoE
         called in an artillery fire mission.

301000H Assumed OPCON CoB 1stBn 1stMarines.

301130H CoE vicinity XD 874382 while searching the area to the west
         of its defensive position found 1 7.62mm heavy machine gun
         with spare barrel and ammo, 1 7.62 light machinegun (RPD)
         with 2 magazines, 4 AK-47's, 21 blocks of TNT with blasting
         caps, 11 AK-47 magazines, 1 RPG round and 500 rounds of
         assorted ammunition.

301815H CoG vicinity XD 864399 received 4 incoming artillery rounds
         from the southwest while friendly artillery was firing and
         requested counterbattery fire from Khe Sanh.

301950H CoE vicinity XD 874382 received 5 rounds of incoming 82mm
         mortar fire. An artillery countermortar mission fired into
         XD 866375 made enemy mortar cease fire. The action resulted
         in 3 USMC WIA non medevacs.

310020H   CoE vicinity XD 874383 received 1 RPG round from east and
1 rifle grenade from north of night defensive position.   Enemy
movement detected to west and south of perimeter.   Fired night
defensive fire with 81mm mortar and 105mm artillery.

310400H   CoE vicinity XD 874382 received a ground attack from 4 di-
rections on their defensive position by 6 NVA with small arms,
RPG's and mortar fire (60mm and 82mm).   CoE replied by firing
night defensive and final protective fires.

310615H   CoB 1stBn 1stMar vicinity XD 866391 observed 4 NVA at XD
866388.   Artillery mission fired.

310740H   CoF 2ndPlat vicinity XD 862392 with 2 tanks received 3 130mm
rounds from direction of Co Roc.   Artillery counterbattery
fired from Khe Sanh.   Results of enemy fire 2 USMC WIA
(1 priority and routine).

310840H   CoE vicinity XD 874382 received 2 incoming 82mm mortar rounds
and replied with artillery defensive fires.

310850H to 311300H   CoB 1stBn 1stMar vicinity XD 871392 while advancing south from Route #9 received heavy small arms fire
and RPG rounds from estimated reinforced NVA platoon in
spider holes.   CoB returned fire with small arms fire and
consolidated position.   Results of action were 8 USMC KIA,
22 USMC WIA, 8 NVA KIA and 1 NVA POW.

311050H   CoF 2ndPlat vicinity XD 862392 with tank in direct support
killed 8 NVA attempting to withdraw to west.

311100H   CoB 1stBn 1stMar vicinity XD 871392 captured 1 NVA.

311110H   CoE 2ndBn 1stMar vicinity XD 865389 moved into position on
CoB 1stBn 1stMar west flank.

311115H   NVA POW is returned to LZ HAWK.   POW claims to be a member of
302 Regt, 308 Division.   POW states 1 NVA platoon (rein) is
in contact with CoB 1stBn 1stMar.

311130H   Artillery and air missions are called in on enemy positions
vicinity XD 868387.

311150H   CoE vicinity XD 874382 while searching outside of defensive
positions found 19 NVA KIA.

311245H   CoE vicinity XD 874382 received 3 rounds of 60mm mortar fire
from the east and replied with 60mm mortar and 105mm artillery
countermortar fire.

INDEX